SIN BOLDLY!

Dr. Dave's Guide to
Writing the College Paper

PROPERTY OF
SENECA COLLEGE
LEARNING COMMONS
SENECA@YORK

Dr. David R. Williams

PERSEUS PUBLISHING
Cambridge, Massachusetts

Also by David R. Williams

Wilderness Lost: The Religious Origins of the American Mind, Susquehanna U.P. 1987

Revolutionary War Sermons, Scholars Facsimiles, 1981

Many of the designations used by manufacturers and sellers to distinguish their products are claimed as trademarks. Where those designations appear in this book and Perseus Publishing was aware of a trademark claim, the designations have been printed in initial capital letters.

Copyright 1992, 1994, 2000 © by Dr. David R. Williams

All rights reserved. No part of this publication may be reproduced, stored in a retrieval system, or transmitted, in any form or by any means, electronic, mechanical, photocopying, recording, or otherwise, without the prior written permission of the publisher. Printed in the United States of America.

A CIP record for this book is available from the Library of Congress.
ISBN 0–7382-0370-X

Perseus Publishing is a member of the Perseus Books Group.

Find us on the World Wide Web at http://www.perseuspublishing.com.

Perseus Publishing books are available at special discounts for bulk purchases in the United States by corporations, institutions, and other organizations. For more information, please contact the Special Markets Department at HarperCollins Publishers, 10 East 53rd Street, New York, NY 10022, or call 1–212–207–7528.

Text design by Jeff Williams
Set in 11-point Janson Text by Perseus Publishing Services

First printing, June 2000
1 2 3 4 5 6 7 8 9 10—03 02 01 00

APPRECIATION

WITHDRAWN

This book originated out of my desire to avoid wasting too much time teaching grammar and writing in my literature classes at George Mason University. Eager to spend more time with Jonathan Edwards and Ken Kesey and less with punctuation, I began to place short jeremiads on reserve in the library. When I discovered that students were xeroxing (yes, "xeroxing," so sue me) these papers at a dime a page, I decided to print my own copies of the entire collection and sell them in the campus bookstore to make a buck. That booklet, *Making It or Faking It*, (now a collector's item) became a word-of-mouth success, used even in composition courses, and I was persuaded to expand the text and to try for a larger market.

What followed was a self-published version then titled *Sin Boldly!*, priced at a provocative $6.66, a personal triumph but a marketing disaster. Bookstore chains will not even look at self-published books, nor will the media review them. Luckily, Perseus Publishing, with access to the corridors of capitalism, had the wisdom to pick up the copyright and publish the edition you now hold in your hands.

I therefore owe my students at George Mason the most. Their horrendous mistakes were my inspiration. Several friends and colleagues also helped to get me organized and to keep me working. Suzanne Melancon was the first professional writer to take my project seriously. Kathy Mitchell was the second. Roger Lathbury and Joyce Greening also contributed significant advice, as did my son Nathan. Kudos also to my agent, David Miller, *sine qua non*, without whom nothing. The moral encouragement provided by a host of others can best be exemplified by the words of Dr. Bruce Levy who wrote me from Texas saying, "Let's face it: writing courses suck. They know it; we know it. The only way to win them over is to admit to the truth right off the bat."

I may be bats, but here's the truth, at least as I see it.

Bullitt

When I walk down the street
and see you fellas
wearing your ankle boots and

very

angry

belts,

That's when I know,
That is when I understand,

that Steve McQueen
will never
go out of style.

And these beautiful boys
ask me,

"Man, are you just one of those
stoned writers,

writing one of those
stoned things?"

And I say,

"baby-

my man-

my child-

your mag wheels
are perfection."

—Perri Pagonis, 1999

CONTENTS

INTRODUCTION
What It's All About

Tired of correcting the same mistakes—even in senior papers—
year after year, hoarse and in danger of developing throat cancer
from endless repetition of the same rules, tired even of my own
lame jokes and pathetic attempts to humorize grammar and the
writing process, at long last frustrated by the inability of far too
many obtuse students to grasp the words of wisdom I have
shouted at them through the apparently impenetrable air, I am
here casting off all pretense and committing to paper the real
rules and regulations that have guided me for years as I grade
student papers. Note that many of these rules apply equally well
to the writing of exams or any other project. In any case, they
should certainly help you in your quest for the dearly desired
grade you think you deserve.

Many of you, with some justification, are convinced that the
rules of composition and grammar are a crock, that they are
petty and irrelevant beyond belief, and that the only reason English professors insist upon them is to exercise one brief and feeble moment of power in their otherwise bleak and powerless
lives. There is some truth to that. There is even a school of
thought within the English-teaching profession that views
grammar as a tool of imperialism, a way for white male culture
to impose its values upon others and make them conform to a
value system that keeps white males in command. There may be
something to that too. And of course there are those who arro-
gantly reject learning such writing rules, knowing for sure that

they will waltz into the executive suite of daddy's firm or will so quickly rise from salesperson to CEO that they will always have a secretary to correct their mistakes for them.

Assuming all this is at least in some part true, doesn't that make it all the more important for you to wield the tools of power rather than be at the mercy of someone else's knowledge? There will always be power and there will always be symbols of it. Knowledge of correct grammar and the ability to write are symbols of this power. I can think of no better symbol of power than literacy. Would you prefer the sword? The aristocratic title? An ugly gold medallion on eight gold chains? A Lincoln Continental? An AK–47? Yourname.com? Since we live in a competitive society in which the struggle for survival is primary, power exists, and power will have its symbols. Literacy is a far better tool and symbol of empowerment than any other, even money.

Historically, the teaching of grammar arose as a deliberate effort to provide arbitrary rules to which all people who aspired to middle class gentility could conform. It was thus a means of taking one of the weapons of power away from a hereditary feudal elite and making it available to all the people. It was part of the eighteenth-century revolt against aristocratic privilege, against a world in which a member of the gentry merely by being a member of the gentry set the norm for what was right and proper simply by whatever he did. King Louis XV, they say, rarely bathed and stank to high heaven, but as king he set the standard and was not subservient to it. However much you may hate grammar, think how much better a system ours is in which even the lowest peasant can achieve literary equality by learning rules of writing, spelling, grammar, and diction that are available equally to all and that apply equally to all. Andrew Jackson, in the early nineteenth century when Noah Webster was trying to stamp equality upon us, resisted this trend, proclaiming he had no respect for the intelligence of a man who couldn't think of more than one way to spell a word. The elite had a glorious freedom in those days, but Harrison Bergeron is dead, shot down by handicapper general Diana Moon Glampers. *Égalité* has assumed a higher value than *liberté*. We must all become the same; we must all be equal. To achieve that goal, we must all submit to the same rules. The ability to write forcefully, convincingly, grammatically is thus less a tool of privilege than one of the strongest weapons against it. It is the tool that you must have if you are to compete successfully against the spawn of Yale and Harvard.

For those business majors and majorettes out there still not persuaded, let me reveal a secret of one of America's leading business tycoons, a secret that should freeze your souls. In *Minding the Store*, his rags-to-riches story of how he made it to the top of his daddy's business with the help of his daddy's millions, Stanley Marcus, former emperor of the Nieman Marcus merchandising empire, lets slip the revelation that he has what he calls "a personal antipathy." What is this shameful prejudice? Dislike of blacks? Fear of Arabs? Hatred for anything in green polka dots? No, his personal antipathy is for the misuse of the personal pronoun after a preposition. He once broke off an engagement to a beautiful and hopeful young lady who almost landed her millionaire until she said in a moment of unguarded passion that there was such great love "between you and I." Off with her head! And then there was the up-and-coming junior executive who responded to a generous Christmas gift by thanking Marcus for the lovely vase he had sent "to Helen and I." According to Marcus, he never rose any further in the organization and did not last long, and he never even knew why.

If you do not know what wrong these two sinners had committed to justify their being cast out of the garden into the darkness where there is wailing and the gnashing of teeth, then you need the lessons in this little book. Perhaps you are right that the rules of grammar are stupid and arbitrary and that the people who wield them are arrogant and petty. But many of those same stupid, arrogant, petty people are out there wielding power. Someday, one of them may be your boss. One of them may be grading your papers this semester. In the interest of survival, if nothing else, you need to be prepared to meet the challenges of this power. As Jimmy Carter once said, "Life is not fair." Victory goes to those who are prepared to deal with life on its own terms, not in terms of some imagined fairness.

Let us get on with it.

1

Some Really Crude Basics

What Is a College Paper?

Let's admit from the start that by "college paper" we mean a paper for a course in the humanities. The sciences, bless them, have their own peculiar ways of using language that many of us in the humanities find bizarre. Of course, the way some humanists write papers is also beyond belief. One need only pick up any work by one of the adherents of the modern "deconstructionist" school of literary analysis to see how bad academic writing can get. Forget all that academic jargon. Any college paper you write reflects your opinion and should be in whatever style or voice is most comfortable for you. And whether the paper is for the English Department, History Department, Psychology Department, Religious Studies, or any of the many subsets of the social sciences, the rules here outlined generally apply. Even such pseudosciences as economics and business require papers that are written in English and follow the same general rules and procedures as an essay on Emerson.

That said, it is undoubtedly true that you can get away with more colorful and creative—if not downright peculiar—experiments in a paper for a literature class than in one for an economics class. But even this is not guaranteed. Some English professors imagine themselves as supersophisticated, scientifically based apostles of some wacko school of literary analysis and therefore insist on rigidly exact performances, whereas some economists are as loose as the proverbial goose. And some of the best scientists write not in science-ese but in clear human language. Reading Freudians is an exercise in despair and confusion; reading Sigmund Freud himself is a delight. There is a reason for this.

The historian Barbara Tuchman has said that the ability to write well implies the ability to think well. Great minds think and write clearly; secondary minds get confused; inferior minds tie themselves in knots pretending they understand what they clearly can't even grasp. People who understand what they are talking about write in clear simple language intended to communicate ideas from one mind to another. This is because they have ideas and want to communicate them. People who do not have a clear idea of what they are talking about try to hide their confusion behind an ink cloud of obscure verbiage. And some superior snots write not to communicate but to impress people with how smart they want us to think they are.

Do not, therefore, be afraid to say what you think in plain, simple English. To the truly literate, the use of excessively pompous and complex language indicates cowardice and ignorance, not intelligence. If you cannot understand your textbook, do not despair; the fault may well be the writer's, not yours. In contrast to European intellectuals with their aristocratic heritage, the best American writers from the very beginning gloried in what we call "the plain style." Our greatest American books offer not clouds of baroque rhetoric but simple American speech. Think of the dialect in *Huckleberry Finn*, the direct sentences of Ernest Hemingway, the penetrating boldness of James Baldwin, and be not afraid. As Emerson so wonderfully said in that most American of essays "Self-Reliance," "Speak your latent conviction and it shall be the universal sense."

The college paper is assigned to determine how well you have mastered the course material, how well you have understood the significance for good or ill of that material, and how well you can write about it. Whether for history, English, or whatever, the requirements of good arguments, good evidence, and good communication are essentially the same. These are the requirements on which this book is focused.

Format and Length

Leave all your plastic binders in Miss Hodgebottom's fourth-grade classroom. They fall apart, scattering pages to the breeze or leaving them to be scrunched up in the bottom of my book bag. The binders feel like slimy death; they are an expensive environmental disaster. Simply staple an 8 1/2 x 11 white title page to the front of your paper.

This title page should have a title in the center about a third of the way down. The title should not be in quotation marks unless it is a quotation. It should not be underlined unless it is also the title of a published work. It should say something. "Paper #2" is not a title. In the lower right-hand corner of this title page should be your name, the date, and the name and number of the class.

Do not repeat the title on the first page. The first page of text should begin at the top as any other page does. Nor should you begin the first page halfway down the paper as if there had to be room for a title that isn't there. We professors know padding when we see it. And for the love of Gaia, do not include blank pieces of paper at either the beginning or the end. Play your tricks of illusion with words. I am constantly amused at the students who try to hide their papers in the middle of the pile when they are turning them in, as if we teachers never read the things. We do. You can't hide from us. And when we get to yours, we will realize with surprising speed that the thick paper handed in was padded by empty sheets on either side. Once so alerted, we will then be on the lookout for padded paragraphs too.

The paper must be typed—or whatever the verb is for word processing. No, we do not accept neat handwriting. An absolute universal requirement is that you double space. We can recognize triple and even two-and-a-half-line spacing, so don't get cute. Double spacing gives us room to write our penetrating critiques of your mistakes between the lines. We need all the room we can get.

Standard margins are an inch and a quarter on the sides, an inch and a half top and bottom. Each page should be numbered.

I prefer the numbers at the top right, out of the way, to leave room for my pithy comments.

The length of the paper, of course, should be part of the assignment. If you are not sure, do not be afraid to ask. If you don't know, chances are very good that others don't know. The rest of the class and the teacher will thank you for clearing up the confusion. An assigned length of two to three pages does not mean one page and a line at the top of the second. It means at least two full pages with the possibility of spillover onto a third. Note that we teachers hate to discourage eager students, but few of us are thrilled to see papers several pages longer than the assignment calls for. Learning to be concise is a major part of learning to write. We are glad you have something to say, but keep it under control please. With perhaps forty four-page papers to grade before tomorrow, we are faced with at least 160 pages to read and edit before dawn. Being able to put yourself in the other guy's or gal's sneakers is a universal requirement for success in any endeavor.

I often do not give page lengths, thereby creating great anxiety, to which I respond by reminding fretting students of the fellow who asked Abraham Lincoln how long a man's legs should be. "Long enough to reach the ground," was his wise response. Your paper too needs to be long enough to carry the body of the text, no more, no less. This refusal to be specific causes problems for me as well, but by giving eight-page assignments to students with four pages worth of knowledge, we professors work against our own instructions. We say, "be brief," "be concise," "don't waste words," and we make fun of bureaucrats who write thirty-page memos on how to buy a doughnut. Then we give out assignments that force many students to learn how to turn four pages of information into eight pages of words. By doing this, we are in fact inadvertently teaching the very excess of verbiage we claim to abhor. Instead, I say, define your topic, establish your argument, present the evidence for this argument, rebut objections, and bring it all to a resounding conclusion. To do all this should take at least four or eight or twenty or whatever the number of pages that may have been assigned. If you think you can do it in fewer than the minimum required, may

Allah be merciful. If you require a bit more, I'll try to understand. Do the best job you can.

Timing Counts!

In graduate school one semester, taking a seminar on William Faulkner from the great Hyatt Waggoner, I had the opportunity to shock a young classmate. She and I and a fellow student were walking along the brick sidewalk outside of class talking about the term papers we had been assigned. Suddenly, she turned and stopped us both in our tracks demanding, "Wait a minute! Are you guys actually saying that you intend to get these papers in on the assigned date?" He and I gave each other puzzled looks and shrugged. She stomped off in a fury saying, "I never heard of such a thing. Why, I've never handed in a paper on time in my life. What are you guys trying to pull?" She didn't return the following semester. He and I are now up to our keisters in sophomore papers.

Deadlines are meant to be taken seriously, not absolutely, but seriously. You are going to have to sit down at some point and do the work, so you might as well determine to do it at the first opportunity instead of the last. There'll be plenty of time for procrastination in the grave. I wish I had the gall of Harvard's late great Alan Heimert. He once assigned us a term paper to be handed in on April 18. After giving us that date, he drummed his fingers on the table, looked up at the chandeliers, then sighed, "Okay, if you develop pneumonia and your dog goes into labor, I suppose I have to let you have an extra week. There, you've got until the twenty-fifth." Then he gritted his teeth, drummed some more, and said, "All right, all right, if the government is overthrown and you have to march on Washington to save the republic, I guess I'll have to give you one more week. There! Do not ask for any more extensions. I've given you an absolute deadline and two extensions. If you can't get it in by May first, forget it!"

Still, some students will insist on making excuses and requesting extensions. One of the problems with this is that we teachers have heard them all. I always tell my sophomores at the beginning of my survey course to kiss their grandparents good-bye before the final, since so many of them seem to kick off that week. Even if there is a death in the family, you need to grit your teeth and get on with life. How long can a funeral take, anyhow?

We teachers get to be a pretty hard-hearted, cynical bunch. Once a sexy young female from Iran came up to me before the midterm, stood altogether too close, and oozed that she would do "anyzing" for an A. When I suggested that she work harder, she burst into tears and confessed she had a problem. She was in the United States, she said, on a grant that required her to get straight A's. If she lost the grant, she would have to drop out of school. If she had to drop out of school, she would lose her student visa and have to return to Iran. Since her father had supported the Shah, if she returned to Iran, she would surely be shot. "Well, guess you really had better work harder," I said. She left in a snit. A week later she was back with another story. This time, she said, she would tell me the truth. She had been exaggerating before, but the truth was that her husband was paying her tuition. He did not believe women should go to college, but if she wanted to go on his money, she had to make straight A's or he would beat her. I believed her that time for some reason, but my answer was the same: Work harder.

How Much Work Do I Have to Do?

Do not even contemplate trying to write the paper in one draft unless it is already 3:00 a.m. of the morning the paper is due and you are so far gone that you don't care what grade you get as long as the assignment is accepted. The first draft is always just a rough sketch of possibilities.

The very act of writing can itself be liberating. The rough first draft may well be nothing more than a page or two of hastily scribbled impressions. If you have any interest or curiosity at all, whether negative or positive, about a specific character or phrase or event, begin describing it. You will be amazed how soon ideas begin to flow. But under no circumstances should you think of this first effort as any more than the jotting down of rough preliminary notes.

If the first draft, then, is barely comprehensible, the second draft is your best working paper. This is written once you have a pretty good idea of what you want to do. It is the skeleton of what will become your final paper. It is also the hardest one to write. Do not worry here about perfection, for this is also the draft that you next must comb over carefully to correct logic and organization, to note where better evidence is called for or has been left out, or where the argument has wandered off the path. The third draft then comes close to being your finished paper, but this is the copy that needs to be examined closely for typos, grammatical mistakes, misspellings, and other last-minute problems.

Ideally, then, your fourth draft should be your final paper. Okay, laugh, but at least you've been told.

2

Choosing a Topic and Telling Your Story

K.I.S.S.

Ray Kroc, the founder of McDonald's, had in his office a sign reading "K.I.S.S.," which, he was glad to tell anyone, meant "Keep It Simple, Stupid." "Simple" does not have to mean simpleminded. Keeping it simple means avoiding the complexity of too many competing, confusing factors. This applies to choosing a paper topic as well as writing a sentence or running a business.

Pick one topic, one argument, that is finite, limited, and can be defined. Do not try to explain everything; it can't be done. Even if you think you know everything, avoid the temptation to put it all in every paper. We college professors do not simply skim the page searching for the magic words that get awarded "points," which we then add up to determine the grade. We actually want a coherent essay, not a bushel of babble. Narrow in on a specific question or problem or character. Pick a word, a phrase, an image, or an event. Ask a specific question: "Why does the author use this particular word or image in this paragraph?" "Why did the Americans in Texas declare their independence in 1836 instead of 1835?" "Why does Jesse Jackson prefer the term 'African American' to 'Afro-American' or 'black'?"

Your analysis of that specific question can then widen to include the larger problems of the text, or of life. Begin with your specific fact or quote or problem and then expand to the larger contexts, first of the work under consideration, then of the author and his or her world, and then, if you are feeling ambitious, of the cosmic whole. But do not leave us floating in outer space. Keep the original rock from which you started in sight and be sure to return to it at the end.

When you do not have to answer the question of what the entire text is all about, the problem of choosing a topic is considerably simplified. You do not have to "understand Faulkner" or "the causes of the Great Depression" or "the meaning of existence" in order to write a sophomore paper. Begin with whatever interests you, even if it is only a single person or phrase or event.

And speaking of stupid, boycott all the Cliff's and Monarch and other shortcuts to an easy C that can be found all too easily in every college bookstore. Many of these can also be found on professors' bookshelves. We read them too. Some of us (may Allah be merciful) write them. At the very least, we eventually come to recognize key sentences because of the many times innocent undergraduates have repeated them. I even had one lamebrain student list the Monarch Notes edition of a text in his bibliography.

The biggest problem with these notes is not that they save you from having to work or even think, but that they are altogether simpleminded when not outright wrong. They are written for consensus. That is, they represent the lowest common denominator of opinion about any given text, and that bar is pretty low. Their generalities are about as insipid as you can get, for the simple reason that any opinion we academics all agree on must necessarily be pretty vague. Think of a politician who has managed to run for president offending neither the AFL-CIO nor the *Wall Street Journal*, neither Louis Farrakhan nor the ACLU, neither the right-to-lifers nor NOW. This person may have no enemies but won't have any friends either. When I teach *Moby Dick*, after spending considerable effort unveiling many of the complex layers of significance in the chapter "The Whiteness of the Whale," if I have any time left at the end of class, I read the banal comments found in one of the standard crib notes. Most of the students get the point.

We teachers also know about the wonders of the Internet and occasionally check out sites like www.schoolsucks.com. Resist the temptation to hand in someone else's work as your own. We have access to software that scans all the texts on the Net and locates plagiarized phrases and sentences as well as paragraphs. After I told my composition class last semester about this new software, a stunned silence filled the room until one student meekly asked, "Is that software up and running yet?"

Brainstorming

Whether you have no idea or even if you begin with a good idea, the very act of writing can itself somehow be liberating. It can break open the dams in the mind. Psychiatrists often recommend to their patients who are blocking that they try writing out their thoughts because this process often helps break up those dams. Ideas occur to the writer that would not occur if he or she were not already pouring words onto the page. One idea stimulates another in a stream of association that reaches deep into the subconscious. A trickle of words soon erodes the levee, and before you realize it the Mississippi is pouring through.

Try scribbling across a blank page any impressions, ideas, arguments, irritations, anything that comes to mind in a frenzy of free association. This process is called "brainstorming" and is the way many successful students come up with their paper topics. Discuss the assignment with friends, enemies, random people you run into on the bus, your stuffed armadillo, your pet porcupine, even your family. My best ideas have arisen in opposition to what I have heard others say. Listening to others can be a great aid in helping you define your own take on the subject. Go to the library and check out a book report, journal article, newspaper column, or website on the issue. You may be surprised how quickly responses crystallize in your mind. You may also be surprised by what other readers think is going on. What you at first thought an obvious and commonplace observation barely worth mentioning much less writing a paper about may well turn out to be a unique and brilliant insight all your own. If

you see an elephant on the page, don't be all that surprised if the other students see orangutans and zebras.

Even if you still have no ideas to scribble out, starting a first draft may be a good way to get an idea. Start not with a topic or idea, for you have none. Start instead with a literal description of the subject or one of the characters or the question of the assignment. Since you need to begin with the literal anyhow, try writing a brief summary, in your own words, of the plot or structure of the text. That very act may be all you need to start your mind expanding. Is the text interesting? Do you care about anything or anyone in it? Do you like one character and dislike another? Why? Is that what the author intended? Why? What does this tell you about the author and about yourself? What about the ending? Is it convincing? Is it even an ending? What about the language? What kind of people actually talk like this? Keep fishing around until you feel yourself reacting with an opinion or until you can imagine an opinion whether you are sure if you share it or not. But under no circumstances try to hand in the wandering thoughts of this first draft as if it were a finished essay.

Why Must We Fight?

In anything you write, you need to be making an argument. This doesn't have to be an angry confrontational argument. Nor does it have to be profound. But there must be some point to it all, some message you are trying to get across. If you cannot imagine anyone disagreeing with what you are saying, then your paper is not an argument. A paper saying the sky looks blue on a sunny day is not an argument. A paper arguing against wife-beating or racism is equally pointless. Who would disagree? You need to go beyond safe conventional moralisms and say something. Instead of merely denouncing wife-beating, argue that alcohol taxes ought to be raised to pay for federally funded women's shelters. That'll get you into an argument in any bar in America.

Presenting and then resolving a conflict is the classic approach to writing any paper. Start off with a problem or a question or a

mystery. A body lies mutilated in the biology lab: Whodunit? Lord Cornbury, one of the colonial governors of New York, used to solicit sailors on the docks while dressed in full drag: Why wasn't he ashamed of his behavior? Why can't that wimp Hamlet make up his mind? What complex secrets lie behind the innocent smile of the blonde in the movie? Why is dark always thought of as evil? Remember the Latin phrase *Cui bono*, not Cher's late ex-husband but a question asked of bills introduced into the Roman Senate, "To whom the good?" Who benefits from this? Who is helped by this, and who is hurt, and why? Because we live in a cause-and-effect universe, every aspect of any text, whether historical, literary, or psychological, contains mysteries waiting to be revealed. Despite the arrogant posturing of academics and scientists, psychologists and economists, human behavior is still a complete mystery. Any activity involving human beings is thus loaded with unanswered and often unspoken questions. All you need to do to come up with an argument is to be as innocent and evil as a child who won't stop asking "Why?" Remember that every event and statement is an effect, and that every effect has a cause. If the reason for an author's or a character's words is not obvious, seize that as your opportunity to argue for your own interpretation. Such mysteries need to be solved.

Having a solution to your mystery, or an answer to your question, at the end of the paper is always helpful, but even that is not necessary. To lay out a problem, to ask penetrating questions, to explore some of the possible answers, to report on another person's suggested answers, can by themselves be worthwhile endeavors. But we teachers do want our students to take risks and to try to express opinions of their own.

The worst papers tend to be written by students who are afraid to voice an opinion, who are afraid of being wrong. Don't worry about being wrong. Most of the time, I don't even care what you believe. Remember, this is not indoctrination. We are not here to brainwash you into accepting our beliefs. We are here to teach you how to argue persuasively. A paper is not a scantron test; it is an opportunity for you to get past the mere recitation of facts and show you know how to think. There will be enough time for neutrality in the grave. In the meantime, we are creatures of passion, driven by our likes and dislikes, hopes and fears. Do not be afraid to voice them.

Relativism is the last refuge of the coward. Patriotism, a close cousin of tribalism, is not far behind. Some students, having no ideas themselves, hide in the platitudes of politicians. Other students, equally afraid to voice an opinion, any opinion, try to hide behind the skirts of relativistic rhetoric. True, all people have the right to their peculiar and perverted views, but you also therefore have the right to yours and even the obligation to speak up for them. Once, during my Fulbright year in Czechoslovakia, just after the fall of the Berlin Wall, I asked one young man, educated under Marxism, what he thought the words of a particularly provocative poem meant. He gave me a literal translation as if we were in first-year English. I asked him then what he thought of the poet's idea as stated in the poem. "The poet," he said, "made this statement because it is what he believed. He is saying what he believes because he believes it. That is what I think." I think of that student often. He was brought up in a system in which having personal opinions was considered downright immoral. There was one truth, worked out by the Communist Party, and students were expected to learn it and spit it back. The idea of admitting they had private thoughts, much less speaking them out loud in a public room with an authority present, was frightening to them.

But what excuse do American students have for hiding behind such nonsense? Our system insists on each individual's worth. We teachers want to know what the world looks like from each student's unique perspective. We want all the conflicting opinions to be heard and debated. Yet many students believe that diversity is an excuse not to have an opinion, as if voicing one's opinion somehow threatens other people's rights to theirs. When asked whether a particular statement is right or wrong, these students repeat the democratic belief that everyone is entitled to his or her opinion and that each person's opinion depends on that person's beliefs. "Yes," I throw back at them, "that is true. And what I am asking for is your opinion. Tell me not what is true for everyone else or anyone else; tell me what you personally think. The world is a circus of many acts. Don't sit in the stands watching; join it. No one will send you to the gulag for being different. Indeed, a new and different act may be applauded."

Daring Dissent

Many students complain to me that their other teachers indeed are such bigots that they reward students who reflect their views and banish those who are different to some academic gulag. To get ahead, say these ass-kissing upstarts, you need to learn to get along. On my campus, fraternity brothers openly snicker over the well-known and successful scenario for acing any course taught by a feminist. All they have to do, they tell me, is to start off pretending to be macho and sexist and then, over the semester, gradually come around to her point of view. The teacher thus rewards them not for their writing but for their "intellectual development" and "heightened maturity." Other students say that to argue a conservative point in a liberal's class, or a liberal point in a conservative's class, is sure death. Although I admit that both sides of the political battlefield have some idiotic ideologues who do not know or care about the difference between propaganda and pedagogy, I suspect that in many of these reported cases, the problem is one not of conforming to the hidden or not-so-hidden agenda of the teacher but of failing to acknowledge it. All teachers have agendas; make no mistake about that. But most teachers are happy simply to have their viewpoints acknowledged, not digested and regurgitated.

Dissent from the class agenda is probably a healthy response and deserves respect, since it is always harder to fight the current than to go with the flow. But such dissent carries with it the additional responsibility of bowing toward your opponent before the battle starts. The tactic, which is simple but effective, involves giving the party line a nod in a brief paragraph near the opening of the paper. All you need to do is to say something like,

It is certainly true that Marx predicted the inevitable downfall of capitalism, and the United States as a capitalist country does exhibit many of the contradictions Marx discerned in capitalism. Indeed, some of these contradictions can be found in a close reading of our current text, *The Essential Calvin and Hobbes*. Nevertheless, other forces more than compensate for the failings of capitalism and have promoted development of the many beneficial aspects of American culture.

Then you can press on with whatever points you originally wanted to make.

The real danger with the dissenting paper, and it is one I have run into numerous times, is the failure to provide any evidence that you have paid any attention to any of the class lectures or read any of the texts. That, after all, is a major reason for writing these papers. The grader needs to have some evidence not only that you have opinions of your own but also that you have read and thought about the assigned work. A dissenting argument that never even mentions the class agenda risks being read as an evasion rather than a response. The connection between your argument and the assignment may be obvious to you, but you have the responsibility to make it obvious to the grader. Spell out clearly but respectfully the points of contact and conflict.

Swindler's List

The opposite of the argument paper is what I call the "list paper." This is the way many of you were taught to write English papers back in high school, and let me tell you, you were swindled. In this model of paper writing, a term paper on "Birds in Shakespeare" might identify three birds in *Macbeth*, four in *King Lear*, and five in *A Midsummer Night's Dream*. The topic sentence points out that many different birds are referred to in Shakespeare. The birds are then named and located. A particularly ambitious paper of this sort might even say what the birds are doing in relation to the plot or what significance they seem to have in each play. The conclusion announces proudly that therefore we can see Shakespeare's use of birds. There is no argument, no point, nothing, just a list of birds. Who cares? What difference does it make? Who can argue against it? What has anyone learned? Give me a stupid argument over an empty list paper any day! In a history course, the equivalent of a stupid list paper is a chronological narrative that gives the sequence of events but nothing else: This happened, this happened, this happened, the end. At the very least, explain the order of your list; perhaps a pattern will be revealed that can lead to a meaningful argument. In the social sciences, too, interpretation, analysis, significance, and insight into causation are the ends desired. We need to know that you know the facts, but we are looking for more than that. With a little imagination, any list paper can be turned into an argument. Everything is controversial these days.

A student of mine from Colombia wrote a paper on ethnicity in which he described several of his family's ethnic traits: food, clothing, holiday rituals. The paper was well-written, and the examples were interesting and lively. But it was basically a list and nothing more. Near the end, he mentioned that his mother sometimes called him a "gringo" because he had become so American in his eating habits. I suggested he take that confrontation, put it up front in the topic paragraph, and then reorganize the facts already in the paper around that conflict. He rewrote the paper starting off describing in detail this tension between his family's traditional Colombian lifestyle and his evolution away from it. He was then able to describe dinners and clothing and language as arenas of cultural conflict. The result was a much better, more meaningful paper, indeed, an A. Everyone likes a good fight.

Also, be sure not only that you have an argument but that you have only one argument. If you have two things to say, write two papers, or make one somehow fit into and under the general umbrella of the more important argument. Think of the entire paper-writing project as the organization of an army going to battle. There can be only one battle plan and one top general. A divided command will produce defeat. Line up all of your battalions in an orderly fashion, face them all in the same direction, and charge.

Finding Patterns:
Comparisons and Contrasts

When you set out to choose a topic, you want to be revealing something new and interesting. Often what you should be doing is looking for patterns, patterns of racist or sexist language, patterns of violence, patterns of religious or other cultural imagery, patterns that reveal character or values. The list could go on forever. The mere fact of the parallel or contrast, however, cannot be the argument of the paper. You need to make something of it. What questions do these comparisons and contrasts raise, and what answer might you suggest?

In "The Doubloon," a chapter in *Moby Dick*, several different characters each try to interpret the symbolic meaning of a gold coin stamped with the picture of a rooster, a volcano, and a tower. Each sees something of himself in the coin. Each projects his personal interests onto the coin, until at last the crazy black boy, Pip, says the coin is the ship's belly button, and he recounts the very old joke that if you unscrew your belly button, your buttocks will fall off. If we ever finally understood God's true and final meaning, suggests Melville, then the whole thing might just come to an end, earth and heavens rolled up like a scroll. Better to leave it a mystery.

We humans, however, cannot stop picking at that scab. Ever since Adam ate the apple, we have pursued knowledge regardless of the risk. We look at people and wonder about them; we watch the news and ask what is really going on; we suspect there is something between the lines or behind the text. We notice patterns of behavior and think "aha!" Why does Julie always date men who drink too much? Why is Fred so eager to convince us so often that he hates gays? One of the tricks of writing college papers is learning to look at our everyday behavior as if investigating the outlandish customs of some South Sea island tribe. Like Fox Mulder and Captain Ahab, we insist that the Truth is out there and we cannot rest until we have grasped it, no matter what the cost. What makes us tick, we want to know, and that very wanting is the ticking we would know about. The I wants to look itself in the eye but cannot stand outside of itself to see itself directly. And so we endlessly chase our tails looking for clues to the meaning of it all. The patterns may be within any one text or between several texts, or between texts and television, or texts and politics, or texts and biology or computer science. Such patterns reveal something and thus raise questions that make excellent paper topics. In one of my published papers, I compare the love poetry of Emily Dickinson with Bob Dylan's album "Time Out of Mind" and argue that in each the absent lover is not some human but Christ. Such unexpected, cross-disciplinary parallels are dear to the hearts of humanities teachers.

A close cousin to the comparison paper is the contrast paper. Here, instead of similar patterns, we find differences that are revealing. Most people think that the many blacks who traveled north to Chicago from the south are generally alike, but black migrants from Alabama and those from Mississippi brought with them distinctly different habits and values. Uncovering hidden differences can be just as interesting as uncovering hidden comparisons. Some Baptists dunk and some Baptists sprinkle. Just what is that all about, anyway?

The best approach is to combine these two perspectives to show both comparison and contrast in the same paper and to develop an argument based on each. One of the classic examples of a good comparison-and-contrast essay is Bruce Catton's "Grant and Lee." In this short essay, Catton uses the personal differences between these men to show the differences between the North and the South that led to the Civil War. Each man is portrayed as a representative of his region, and by the time Catton has shown us these two men, we understand why they fought and why both are revered as great Americans.

When I got out of high school, not wanting to rush right into college, I spent time on a tramp steamer crossing the Pacific, the only American gringo in an international crew. At first, I was thrilled at how similar we all were, white and black, European and Asian, Panamanian and Filipino. I came to understand the dreams of one-world universalism and renounced my narrow nationalistic ways. But in time, the 90 percent of ways in which we were all the same came to be taken for granted, and the 10 percent in which we differed loomed larger and larger, like a pebble in one's shoe, until, by the end of the voyage, I came to realize that to be an American was different, and in some ways better, better enough to be worth fighting to defend. Together, the comparison and the contrast told a story.

Freeing the Slaves

That, then, is the next consideration: Your essay must not only be an argument. It must also be a story. In the movie *Amistad*, when the abolitionist Theodore Joadson, played by Morgan Freeman, tries to persuade John Quincy Adams, played by Anthony Hopkins, to take the slaves' case, Adams demands to know, "What is their story?" Joadson doesn't get it at first, so Adams explains that to win the case, he needs to have more than the facts and the law. He must have a compelling story, one that will grab the attention of the court and the public. People respond to stories, not to facts. People prefer movies to the news, and we follow the news only when it is offering a compelling story like the Cold War or Elian. For an entire year, the story of Bill and Monica and the stained dress was all we seemed to hear. The story of the *Amistad* Africans, the "whopping good story" that Spielberg set out to tell, was the story of a group of innocent people sold into slavery, breaking the bonds of captivity, and fighting to become free.

Your paper too must tell a story. Luckily, a good argument becomes a story naturally if organized right. My Colombian student's paper about his gringo eating habits became a story of a family emigrating to a strange land and becoming divided. Would the family accept the new habits, or would they reject their prodigal son? Would he return to his family's table and renounce his new ways, or would he change and become a gringo? Would the family ever come back together again and be as they were in the old country? These problems needing to be overcome turn an otherwise dull list of events into a story. Any question implies a problem. Any problem provides the opportunity for confrontation and resolution, for winners and losers, for a story. Even a memo to the boss about buying paper clips is more successful if told in the form of a story about an employee who wastes two expensive hours because he couldn't find a paper clip at a crucial moment in some task.

For those who think stories are for children or are entertainment or mere embellishment, not fit for the hard realities of the real world, consider money. Dollars by themselves are nothing more than pieces of paper with green ink. Even the government's declaring them to be worthwhile is not what makes them valuable. Government decrees didn't help Confederate money after the Civil War or the German mark in 1925. U.S. dollars are valuable, in New York and in Uzbekistan, because you and I and the guy who runs the corner liquor store believe they are valuable. Stories, not atomic particulars or cold dirty cash, are the foundation of it all. Even our economy is dependent upon all of us believing the same story. Some innocents out there called technicians or "elves" really believe the stock market is controlled by mathematical logic. But as a writer to a Yahoo stock group explained to a neophyte:

> This isn't a reality-based market. It's a story-based market. All you need is a good story about how you are going to make money in the future. Look at eBay or Amazon. CRA and PLUG doubled within two days of articles telling their stories. Were they better companies? No, but more people knew their stories. Meanwhile, big strong companies that ought to do well go nowhere. There's no story about how they are going to take over the world.

If everyone believes the story that a stock is going to do very well, and it does only well, that stock goes down. But if everyone believes the story that the stock is going to do badly, and it does well, that same stock goes up even though the numbers are no different. Only the story is.

Many wonderful literary essays are in fact stories. Both Ralph Ellison and Richard Rodriguez, neither one a white boy from the antebellum South, begin their discussions of *Huckleberry Finn* by telling the stories of their personal encounters with the book when they were young. They tell their stories as a way of telling us what the book means, not just to them but to other people like them, presumably including us. The story of the reading of a book is thus one approach. But the story of the writing of a book, or of any one part of a book, is also full of potential. Sometimes you have to read several works by an author before you can begin to see in the parallels between the texts what story he or she is trying to tell. Sometimes authors themselves are not all that clear on why they are compelled to write as they do, and so literary critics come along and like psychoanalysts uncover their stories for them. And often, like the characters in Melville's "Doubloon," we read our own personal stories into the narrative of the text. There is nothing wrong with this; indeed, it is all but inevitable. The secret is to do it successfully, that is, persuasively. Show me that your story and the text really do speak to one another. Show me how the mirrors in the text taught you something about yourself.

End with a Bang

Every song ends on the same note on which it began. Why? Because the mind demands it, which is to say, I haven't a clue. But I do know of a tale about how Bach's son used to wander home from the bars in the wee hours of the morning and play one of his father's pieces right up to the last note, then abruptly stop and drag himself to bed. The elder Bach, so the story goes, would have to get up, put on his nightclothes, and go downstairs and hit that final key before he could hope to get back to sleep. What does the story mean? It means that to create a sense of completion (I refuse to use that trendy term "closure," for there is no such thing, not in this life), a writer has to end his or her paper on the same note on which it began. Since the paper should open with a specific picture or argument or phrase, some echo of that original opening at the end gives the reader a sense that the paper has all been tied up in a nice neat package. Only then can we sleep in peace.

Echoing words from the topic paragraph, however, does not guarantee that the paper actually is tied up at the end. You still need a solid concluding paragraph that wraps up the argument you are making. This conclusion should not bring in new ideas or new evidence. Instead, it should be a completion of what has already been presented. It need not be a peroration, a resounding climax full of sound and fury, but it should, like the opening topic paragraph, grab the attention of the reader. If you cannot think of an ending, you may not have told a story. If you have not told a story, then you may not have had an argument to make. If you get this far, and do not know what to say at the end, perhaps a moment's reconsideration is in order.

Before Plunging In

A word of caution is in order here.

Once you have a rough idea of what you want to write about, you might want to reconsider before you commit yourself. One of the most crucial decisions is being made here, and too precipitous a jump might land you in trouble.

On that tramp steamer returning up the American coast from the South Pacific, after passing through the Panama Canal, we made our first stop in the United States in Charleston Bay for a customs inspection. One of the things the inspectors were looking for was dope, of course. The other crew members were wise to this dance. Since I was the only gringo among the crew, they figured my room would be the last one to be searched. So they decided to hide their stash with me. But when it came to finding a hiding place, they had a rule: Reject the first ten places you think of, even if some of them seem foolproof. The idea was that if we thought of them, so would the inspectors. There was a deliberate rejection of the arrogant assumption that somehow any idea that popped into our heads would not just as easily pop into anyone else's. It was good advice. And the eleventh hiding place was a beaut. As it happened, the inspectors glanced through my doorway, saw that I was white, nodded politely to me, and then ransacked the other rooms. Since they never entered my room, we never found out if our hiding place was a safe one. Nevertheless, the lesson stuck with me. And it applies equally well to the writing of college papers.

Any idea that pops into your head is bound to pop into the heads of almost every other person in the class. There is no such thing as "free will" (see my essay in *Harvard Theological Review*

74:4 [1981] on Jonathan Edwards and B. F. Skinner). We are all products of our environment and our genes. Our differences are due to different contingencies of reinforcement. Our thoughts are not created by us. They come irresistibly out of the depths of the mind. We cannot cause a thought to come before we have already thought it; nor can we stop a thought from coming without first thinking it. Ideas are like other sensations that are sensed by the mind. Just as we hear sounds and see sights, we "think" thoughts. But for some reason, unlike with hearing sounds and seeing sights, we are cursed with the arrogant illusion that we somehow create the thoughts we think. Not so.

Hence, you want to avoid jumping on the first idea that pops into your head. Since you are quite similar to your fellow students, and since you are all in the same classroom environment, the chance of the same ideas popping into each of your minds is very likely. And sure enough, most papers on any given topic in any one class bear a remarkable and boring similarity to stale popcorn. The few papers that are different stand out. They wake teachers up. They impress us. We say, "Here is a student who can think and not just react like some Pavlovian dog." In fact, such students are also reacting, but they are reacting from a more complex level—and they get better grades.

3

In the Beginning . . . Pulling Your Creation Out of the Void

The hardest part of any job is breaking the force of inertia and getting started. For any writer, having to create something on that white piece of paper or that blank computer screen can be a terrifying experience. The black folk artist Dilmus Hall, one of West Virginia's awesome works of nature, shouts with hellfire fervor at anyone within earshot, "You listening to me? You listening to me? God is the creator, yes; he created us in his image, so each and every one of us got the power to create!" Think of him creating works of art out of trash and scrap metal other people tossed aside the next time you find yourself staring into the terrifying white abyss of an empty sheet of paper. Here is a clue to the terror Melville saw in the whiteness of the whale. But if he overcame that terror and produced *Moby Dick*, then surely you can produce a decent college paper.

Do I Really Need an Outline?

Once you have your topic and your argument, you can begin to write. An outline is helpful, but it does not have to be explicit. Melville may have begun *Moby Dick* with little more than a plan to tell the story of a doomed trip to find something that, when we find it, will destroy us. An adequate outline might be no more than three phrases suggesting a beginning, a middle,

and an end. At its absolute minimum, your final paper will
need only

- a title,
- a topic paragraph with a topic sentence that proclaims
  the argument,
- an explanation of the argument,
- some evidence from the text or texts for the explanation
  of the argument,
- a counterargument that you swiftly demolish,
- perhaps some sense of the larger significance of your
  theme,
- and then a conclusion reasserting the truth of the argument you proclaimed in your opening paragraph.

Outside material such as scholarly articles, book reviews, and
other books on the same topic certainly add to the quality of the
argument and should be included. But you might survive without them. This is your most basic outline. Other models certainly suffice.

Puritan sermons consisted of a fairly rigid three-part outline:
text, explication, uses—a good model to follow. The "text" can
be anything from a line of Scripture to a natural object or event
like an earthquake. Presenting this can take some detail. "Explication" is the full interpretation of the text, its history, its context, the definitions of the terms, even the different
interpretations possible. But in "uses" (sometimes called the
"application") of the text is where the real argument, foreshad-
owed in the topic paragraph, is to be found. This is where the
question "So what?" is answered. This is where the preacher explains why he is bothering to tell us about this text at all, what
relevance it has for our lives. Robert Frost's poems follow this
pattern. First he describes his text, the tuft of flowers or the de-
caying woodpile, then he offers several stanzas of explication. At
the end, the moral points out the message to be derived from it
all. However else you organize your paper, be sure that text, explication, and uses are somewhere there.

Since I tend to think in pictures, I try to have a graphic image of what my argument is going to look like. If I am comparing two points of view or two texts or two personalities, I might imagine a zigzag line going back and forth between them: "On this first point, Marx says this . . . , but Adam Smith says something else. On the second issue, here's Karl again . . . , but along comes Adam with his rejoinder," and so on. This point-counterpoint approach makes for a basic and easy-to-follow outline.

Another picture of the argument might be that of two legions of lawyers in court, each with its evidence and arguments. After an explanatory introduction, we have two to three pages of Catherine MacKinnon's wonderfully strident rhetoric on the date-rape issue; then we have three to four pages of Camille Paglia's colorful prose. After these two blocks, each side gets a chance to refute the other. Then comes another block with our analysis of each or of both together, with appropriate quotations. Finally, we sum it all up for the jurors, treating them respectfully but making sure they understand the points.

If the lawyer metaphor offends you, think of your paper as an army marching to war. You need to have a basic organization, a single purpose, and a unified command. But keep it simple and under control.

What's in a Title?

I highly recommend that you quickly adopt a working title. The title can always change later, but to have a title at the start is to have a guide, a sense of direction, a reminder of what the paper is about. Whenever I get a paper titled "Paper number 2," I know that it is going to be a dud, that the writer has nothing to say. "Hamlet: An Analysis of the Play" is not much better. Nor does a title echoing the assignment stir my juices. I want to know what you have to say, not hear my own rhetoric reflected. On the other hand, "Emily Dickinson and Allen Ginsberg: Black Holes of the Mind" makes me want to read the paper. This title suggests the content might be interesting. Like the headlines on the tabloids at the supermarket checkouts, the titles of your papers need to lure the reader inside. I used to say that they need to be sexy, that like a Victorian woman who lifted her skirt to flash a bit of ankle, they need to titillate the reader and make him or her want to see more of what's under the cover. But I have been accused of "sexual harassment" for even suggesting in class that men might be physically attracted to women and vice versa. That is not politically correct, so I will not say it here.

The Topic Paragraph

Your finished paper must begin with a topic sentence in a topic paragraph. On this I insist. Do not slowly build up to the point you are trying to make. I have no patience for long uphill climbs to the peak. I want to be able to view the scene right at the start to get an idea of where I am and where I am going. After you have introduced your thesis or argument as boldly as you dare, then in the second paragraph you can go back and fill in the biographical details or whatever else is absolutely necessary. A paper on the assassination of John F. Kennedy should not begin with Kennedy's being born unless some new revelation about the time or place of Kennedy's birth is in fact the topic of the paper.

Often in composition classes (I tend to be more lenient in literature classes), I will cross out the first one or two paragraphs entirely and tell the student to begin with the second or third paragraph and never look back. It often takes students that long or longer to get to their points. Such warm-ups are necessary; they're akin to how an orchestra tunes up before a concert, but the audience does not necessarily want to listen in. Begin like Beethoven's Ninth with a powerful statement that will capture everyone's attention. Be sure that all of the topic paragraph flows naturally from that topic sentence. Do not try to sneak in some of your supporting details or arguments here; these should be reserved for later paragraphs. That is what the rest of the paper is for. A one-word hint or a lively verb that indicates the direction you are taking is great, but keep it short. Remember that your topic paragraph (indeed every paragraph) must have only one topic, which is stated in the topic sentence. Remember also that the topic must be some sort of argument. Come out fighting!

Topic Sentences

Hitting the ground running may be a cliché, but it makes good strategic sense. Students in my classes soon learn to avoid "there was," "it is," and all the other intransitives that go nowhere and do nothing. A gerund (a verb with an "ing" ending) or an infinitive ("to" plus a verb) makes a good opener because a verb is an action word. Putting the conflict that is the heart of the paper's argument up front shows the reader that in your paper, unlike in so many others, something will happen. This can also be done with a quote or with an anecdote. If you are arguing against abortion, begin with a battered fetus. If you are arguing for legal abortion, begin with the bleeding body of a girl who was the victim of a back-alley abortionist. You do not have to state your argument blatantly; you can show it. Journalists like their lead sentence or paragraph to contain the five W's: who, what, where, when, and why. Not all of these can be easily forced into every opening sentence, but having as many as possible does help orient the reader.

Not only must the topic sentence introduce the theme, but it also must anticipate the action of the paper. Don't give everything away, but do let the reader know something is coming. Start off a paper on your pit bull, Fluffy, by saying, "The day we brought him home from the pound, I didn't realize what those tiny little teeth would someday be able to do to a man's arm." Unlike an opening sentence that merely declares how cute the little puppy was, this sentence keeps the reader going, waiting for the blood. An autobiographical paper that begins "I was grounded for the first time at the age of five" lets the reader know that more times are to come. Think of the ways TV shows and movies construct suspense to keep you from changing the channel, and see if you can apply those lessons to your paper.

Some writers prefer to place their topic sentence at the end of the paragraph on the grounds that the ends of sentences and paragraphs leave the strongest impression. Joan Didion is a master of this style. But she has been working on her writing for many decades. Most college students would do better to get to the point ASAP. More often than not, the topic sentence will be rewritten after the first draft is done and you have a better idea of what you are saying. So don't be like my friend in graduate school who wasted thousands of sheets of paper struggling to create the perfect opening line only to give his doctoral thesis up in despair and quit. If he had begun with an inferior sentence and the resolve to go back and improve it later, he might not be selling Disney cable subscriptions door-to-door today.

Keep the Flow Going

Within the paper it is important to keep the argument flowing smoothly. Remember, your absentminded reader might well get lost. Do not turn your back on her, or as you ascend you will find she has been left far behind contemplating some bush by the side of the path. Hold her hand by gently reminding her where you are and where you are heading. Do this by repeating key words or phrases that will keep both her and you on track. Knowing how to do this without overdoing it or becoming patronizing is part of the art of good writing. If, in a paper on racism, you are forced to spend several paragraphs outlining Marx's theory of surplus capital or Freud's analysis of infantile repression, be sure to remind your reader occasionally why this side trip is necessary so she will not think you have simply lost your way. Reassure your poor befuddled reader that you still have the map you started with in mind.

Be sure to use transitions between paragraphs. It may be perfectly clear to you why you are now suddenly talking about what may seem to be a different subject. But it may not be at all clear to your reader. If your next paragraph is offering additional supporting material, write "Furthermore" or some other phrase that suggests this. If you are offering an opposing bit of evidence, write "But" or "Nevertheless" or some other clue to help your reader know what you are up to. It is often a good idea to include a key word from the previous paragraph at the beginning of your new paragraph. Such transition words are important bridges and make the passage between paragraphs much smoother. Do not expect your readers to have the patience to wait and see how it all eventually comes together. We have all watched too much television and expect instant gratification. Do not keep us readers too long in suspense, or you are in danger of losing us to a different website or another channel.

Sentences and Paragraphs

Since you are beginning to write, you should consider the basic tools of the trade. The *sentence* is the hammer you use to drive your points home. Each blow must hit a nail. Each sentence must communicate a thought clearly from your mind to that of your reader. Disorganized jumbles of words and phrases cannot do this. Only when the words are arranged in a logical order with a subject and a verb is a complete thought expressed. The presence of both a subject and a verb is what defines a sentence. Be sure that every sentence has each. Be sure the subject and verb agree. Be sure the thought is clear. Sentences can be long or short, complex or simple, but each must contain a clear sense of an actor and some action. Start each sentence with an upper-case letter; end each sentence with a period, question mark, or exclamation point. This stuff is basic. Get it right.

Sentences should be varied. Writing the entire paper in short, choppy sentences will make you sound like Mr. Rogers reading *Dick and Jane*. But long, elaborate sentences full of subordinate clauses and other complexities one after another will wear down your reader and produce an impenetrable thicket of words instead of clear, concise prose. There is no happy middle ground here. Mediocre is boring; even God spits the lukewarm out of his mouth. Go back and forth between both styles.

The *paragraph* is the next unit of organization. It needs to be disciplined and unified as if it were a mini-essay all by itself. That is, each paragraph needs to be organized around its own topic and must begin with its own topic sentence, a sentence that in one way or another introduces the particular topic that distinguishes that paragraph. The remainder of each paragraph, the logic and evidence that back up the topic, must flow naturally from the topic sentence that heads it. One insight per paragraph is the rule. By "insight," I mean something you must take a risk to say, something a reasonable person would want explained, explored, or defended. You will know you are doing it right when you feel exposed and doing it wrong when you feel safe and dull.

If you find that three different ideas seem to be competing in your paragraph, you have two ways to correct the problem. The first is to divide the paragraph into three separate paragraphs, each elaborating on one of the three points. If you lack enough to say to support an entire paragraph for each of these three points, an alternative is to go back to the beginning of the paragraph and create a new umbrella topic sentence that says something like "Three basic arguments can be presented for the belief that Madonna is in fact the reincarnation of Mary, the mother of Jesus Christ." Your three separate points are now subsets of the topic sentence at the beginning of the paragraph. If you can't imagine a topic sentence that would cover everything in your paragraph, you'd better break up the paragraph. If an idea or piece of evidence does not belong with the rest of the paragraph, move it to where it does belong, create a new paragraph for it, or leave it out.

Be Specific

Some teachers like students to begin with general statements and to end with specific examples. Some like papers that begin with the specifics and let the generalities flow from them. No teachers like papers that are all generalities, and only teachers of poetry relish papers that rely on specific images without any explanatory generalizations. Personally, I prefer papers that begin with specifics, that contain many specifics, but that do have occasional generalities when needed to make the point perfectly clear to the reader. As I warned you before, it's never safe in a college paper to let the reader infer the point; we professors read too many papers that have no point. We are always suspicious of papers that seem to be implying something but can never quite spit it out. Leave the artsy stuff for your first published novel, or for graduate school at the very least.

By specifics, I mean facts, dates, quotations, information, stories. I want to see pictures in my mind as I read. I cannot comprehend pure abstraction. Idolatrous as it may be, I would clothe even the deity in some sort of form in order for my feeble mind to have something to imagine. If *Newsweek* runs an article comparing education in Russia and the United States, it will not begin with a generality like "Education in Russia is dogmatic and regimented, whereas education in the United States is permissive and value-free." Instead, it will begin with a word-picture that the reader can see, specific images that bring the comparison to life: "In his fourth-grade class in Moscow, ten-year-old Gorby Snititovitch sits down quickly after carefully reciting his multiplication tables and the ten most important obligations of a good citizen to the state and its leaders. Meanwhile, in Fairfax, Virginia, ten-year-old Stephen Whitebread draws pictures of airplanes in the margins of his math book while his teacher beams with pleasure at such examples of spontaneous creativity."

Like a political cartoon, the picture says it all. But to be safe, *Newsweek* will then go on to state the generality illustrated by the comparison of the two images. The article will include facts from the two schools, number of hours spent at different specific tasks, the level of instruction reached in a school year, number of pages of literature read and discussed, and so on. The writer will also incorporate quotations, lively word-pictures themselves that add color and veracity to the points being made. Even the generalities drawn from the specifics will not be allowed to stand without some more specific backing. Education experts or cultural anthropologists will be cited to back up the truth of the comparison and the significance that can be drawn from it.

Specifics give a paper more authority. A student who writes that he can say anything he wants because this is a free country is less convincing than one who writes that he can say anything he wants because freedom of speech is guaranteed by the Constitution of the United States. But the student who writes that she can say whatever she wants because the First Amendment to the Constitution guarantees that the government can make no law "abridging the freedom of speech" of the people will be the one everyone listens to with respect. She sounds as if she knows what she's talking about. Why? Because she was the most specific.

Being specific applies to whatever kind of paper you are writing. In a history paper, give the most detailed facts possible. Be sure to cite where you found them. Don't paraphrase what King George said if in fact you can quote a phrase or a line from the old tyrant himself. If you are analyzing Martin Luther King, quote the specific words that prove whatever point you are making. Do not talk in generalities about his "noble Southern rhetoric" or his "Baptist style" without also showing me examples. Do not refer to e. e. cummings's "peculiar punctuation" without providing evidence. For all you know, I may find his punctuation perfectly normal and may therefore be sitting here wondering what you are talking about. If you are looking for ways to stretch your paper to the required length, you might even provide more than one example. But do not overdo it. Two or three are plenty.

In addition to citing specific examples taken from the text or from outside research, relating personal anecdotes from your own experience can be an excellent way to illustrate whatever point you are trying to make. To the frustration of journalists and scholars, Ronald Reagan used personal anecdotes instead of facts to communicate quite successfully with the public. But be careful. We scholars—and we professors all like to call ourselves "scholars"—do like to see a few hard facts, real quotes, or statistics among the personal story-telling. Anecdotes can illustrate but can't substantiate.

4

Choosing a Voice

Whom Must You Pretend to Be?

Part of the choice you have to make when you choose a topic is the voice in which the paper is to be written. Voices are extensions of people, and, like people, they have different viewpoints and opinions. None is objective. Thus the topic of your paper will be closely related to the voice in which you choose to write. A paper denouncing the awful sexism of Randle McMurphy in *One Flew Over the Cuckoo's Nest* will have a different voice from one analyzing the metaphors of flowers in Emily Dickinson. Too many students take for granted that any college paper has to be in a pompous professorial objective voice. This is a mistake. In an effort to prevent this horror, some professors go to great lengths to stress the importance of writing in your own voice. This is good advice, but it can be a bit simplistic. Most of us, after all, have several different voices. We speak one way to our peers, another way to our boyfriends or girlfriends, and a different way altogether to the cop who pulls us over on the highway. Which one is truly us? And in this paper, which audience are we trying to reach?

Despite what you may have heard in the school yard, very few of us teachers really want to see students assume our voices and regurgitate our words back at us. When we do get such papers, we carefully turn the pages with rubber gloves and breathe through our mouths to avoid the smell. We are embarrassed. We might sigh and tell ourselves that at least the student was paying attention, and in a well-crafted paper in a well-ventilated room, that might be worth a B. But it is not what we want. We really want each student to draw upon his or her own reading, thinking, experience, and insights and to show us something we have not yet seen. We want our students to use the paper as an opportunity to say what they have to say, to tell their own truths. We want them to teach us something we do not already know.

For this reason, I used to be one of those teachers who require their students to tell the truth, to speak in their most honest voice, to say what they really believed about the subject under consideration and give not a whit about what they thought I wanted them to think. It became apparent, however, that in saying all this, important and true as it was, I was burdening them with the additional responsibility of trying to figure out who they were and what they believed before they could even begin to write the simplest sophomore paper. To make the resolution of the adolescent identity crisis a prerequisite for writing a simple term paper is indeed to throw an all but insurmountable obstacle into the path of the earnest undergraduate. Many students stumble at the threshold, unable to write a word because they haven't the vaguest idea either what they are "supposed" to say or what they personally want to say. No reason exists to be ashamed of this. Anyone who at eighteen is certain he knows what it is all about needs to get a life. I know I did.

Faking Other Voices

So instead I now suggest this to my students: If you are unsure of yourself, then be someone else. Be yourselves if you can, but if you are unable to come up with a good topic of your own, if you are unsure of your personal opinion, then choose a voice. Choose a personality. What person would you like to be? If you cannot come up with a clear idea of what you think about *Moby Dick*, then imagine what a Trotskyite lesbian terrorist gang leader might think, or a capitalist banker, or Michael Jordan, Jesse Jackson, Jesse Ventura, Jesse Helms, or your football coach, or your favorite rap star, or your Yiddish uncle, or one of the characters in the text—anyone but your teacher. The exasperated-professor voice of this book is a good example; in reality, I'm what my friend Gale Waldron calls a "wuss," a softy, really! I sound strict, but I give more A's than I ought to admit.

As a way of introducing the possibility of faking a voice when I teach composition, I ask the students to write a paper describing their most admired relative. Their next paper has to be in the voice of that relative. This is more an exercise in acting than in honesty, but, hell, as Shakespeare said, we are all acting our parts upon the stage anyhow. Sincerity is for saints and mystics, or for liars. Besides, I don't know who you "really" are any more than you do. All I want is a clearly heard voice with a distinct opinion backed up by some facts as evidence for your argument. I also want to be entertained. Don't bore me; ham it up a bit.

The reason I ask for honesty in the first place is not, I confess, because I care all that much about your personal emotional development. I primarily want to read a paper that struts the solid certainty of an honest, heartfelt opinion. Like the reaction I get listening to a speech by Alan Keyes, the good, solid feeling that goes with conviction is what I want, even if I don't agree. The best works of literature may well be brilliant deceptions, as all human endeavors must ultimately be. "All is vanity," said the prophet, and he was right. If you are one of those lucky self-deceived souls who thinks he or she knows something, then good, go for it. Use "your" most honest voice. But if you are still in the wilderness of youthful uncertainty, then "choose a voice." If you can't make it, fake it. That's what most writing is all about. None of us is as good as we can make ourselves sound on paper.

Sin Boldly!

One important point about your adopted voice and its argument: You must at least pretend to believe it. Like Solomon and all great minds that ever contemplated the human condition, Martin Luther was right when he said that all of humankind are sinners and sin in every thought and deed and must necessarily sin, so far are we removed from God. His response was, he declared, to "sin boldly." Do not hide quivering under the bed. Do not shuffle shamefully onto the stage full of abject apologies. Be

assertive, be bold, adopt a self-confident voice. Fake it if you
have to. The cynics may be right. Our worldly institutions and
values may all be relative and artificial constructs like the money
in our wallets or the latest clothing fad. We live in the world "as
if." To some that "if" is a constantly looming threat; to others it's
a challenge.

Consider Ronald Reagan. He had no idea what he was talking
about. He acted out the part of the self-confident leader, and he
got himself elected president twice and was a fairly successful
president despite himself. The only difference between Harvard
students and community college students is that Harvard students think they are right even when they are wrong, and community college students think they are wrong even when they
are right. The amount of prior knowledge or the ability to think
are about the same, believe me. I've been there. The students
who get into Harvard are the ones who adopted (or were given
along with their trust funds) self-confident voices early in their
careers and stuck with them. They are not self-confident because they are smart; they are what we call "smart" because they
are self-confident. So be assertive. Don't be a wimp. The colum-
nist George Will is a very good example, most of the time, of a
fine essay writer. So is that crypto-fascist Pat Buchanan. Who
can forget his description of Republicans deserting Reagan during Irangate as hyenas "heading for the tall grass" or his inflammatory suggestion at the 1992 Republican convention that "we
take back our culture, block by block" or his description of his
followers as "peasants with pitchforks"? What makes these
phrases memorable? He has clear and definite (if misguided)
opinions that provide him with the self-confidence to sin boldly.

So don't quibble and equivocate and hide behind excuses.
Don't begin by saying, "In my opinion . . . ," or "It seems to me
that . . ." These give you away. They say, "It's just little old stupid me saying this and it's probably wrong, so don't hit me,
please." That kind of cringing only brings out the bully and the
sadist in me. I smell fear, and I pounce, pouring red ink like
blood all over the page. Instead, sin boldly! Say "Beyond a
doubt, George W. Bush is a communist dupe and an agent of the
still-dangerous international communist conspiracy readying its

UN black helicopters to herd us all into ditches and kill us like dogs." I know it's you talking; you don't have to tell me. I know it's your opinion; that is obvious. Make the best argument you can backed up by the best evidence and the tightest logic you can muster. Good luck.

Already I can hear what Robert Burns called the "unco' good and the rigidly righteous" bewailing the immorality of such arrogance. I make no apologies. Nor will I claim some higher morality or justifiable excuse for this approach. Biblical prophecy notwithstanding, the meek are not going to inherit the earth, not in this generation, or at least not until the strong are through with it. Besides, sweet reasonableness, more often than not, is a clever disguise for barely concealed self-interest. Writing is a tool of survival and power. As Tom Peters, a management consultant for one of the hot software development firms in the 1980s, once told the *Washington Post*, "In order to do anything interesting on this planet, you've got to be insanely arrogant."

"Arrogant" is probably the right word for it, too. The literary theorists who dominate the academic world in these dark and dangerous times have concluded that everything is socially constructed, that there is no absolute truth. Their hero, Jacques Derrida, is often quoted as having said (albeit in French), "There is nothing outside the text." If this is true, then each of us is a constructed text. Each of us is an act being played upon the stage. There is no Truth outside our constructed texts. We are all faking it anyway, so why worry about sincerity, truth, and all those romantic, essentialist heresies? If the "self" is an invented construction, then your own invention is as real as the social construction you grew up with. It may seem insanely arrogant, but go ahead and choose a voice.

As long as you are being, or pretending to be, arrogant, never announce what it is you are going to do; just do it. Jump in feet first. Don't ever say, "In this paper I am going to show that George Bush is a member of the international communist conspiracy. I am going to make an argument that he did more than any other person to bring about the destruction of the United States by bankrupting the nation in the name of anticommunism. Then I will provide supporting evidence to back up my claim." Such cautious announcements of intent bespeak uncertainty. Instead, simply state your assertion boldly. Then present your argument and your facts. Long-winded introductions are tiresome. They are but doormats. I wipe my feet on them.

The key here is self-confidence, a quality that unfortunately cannot be taught. You need to liberate yourself from the fear of being wrong or the fear of flunking. Emerson in his classic essay "Self-Reliance" says that we are afraid for two reasons: We fear the ridicule of the crowd, and we are terrified we might say something today that contradicts what we said last weekend. But, he warns, "A foolish consistency is the hobgoblin of little minds, adored by little statesmen and philosophers and divines." Students who write careful, cautious, timid papers in an attempt to appease the anger of the arbitrary red pen of the grader will not do as well as those who angrily or boldly or proudly or insanely throw caution to the wind, damn the torpedoes, and charge bravely ahead. We graders like to be entertained, and we like ideas, facts, thoughts. We tend to be those peculiar kinds of people who actually read books for fun, and the kinds of books we like to read are bold and imaginative and original and lively. They are books full of real voices irresistibly alive on the page, voices that teach us something or reveal a new angle.

Dialogue

Writing in an engaging voice is sometimes difficult for the timid. Not ready to dance naked on the stage before the world, these bashful souls can write only in a safe, sane third-person neutral. But even they have another option. They can bring in voices clearly not their own by quoting other people, puppets whom they manipulate for their own purposes. Bringing in such voices in dialogue adds zest to what might otherwise be a monotonous monologue and allows the writer to display some colorful writing without the danger of personal ridicule. After all, the other guy said it, not you. Remember that each new voice gets its own paragraph. Thus, if you have two voices arguing, each new speaker begins a new indented line, even if each is simply shouting,

"Yes, it is."

"No, it isn't."

"Yes, it is!"

This alternative voice also provides a way to bring in counterarguments that question the main voice of the paper, always a crucial element of any successful essay. Think of the best authors you have read, Harriet Beecher Stowe or Charles Dickens for example, and you will realize that much of their success is their ability to create a variety of different characters with wonderful dialogue.

Voices to Avoid

Once you know the voice you want to pretend to be, another warning is in order. Some voices do not succeed as well as others. Without crushing your creativity, I need to point out the political dangers here. If you insist on using an obnoxious voice, do so in such a way that the voice clearly discredits itself. I emphasize "clearly." The mere fact that a voice is obviously, say, racist does not by itself show that the author understands it is objectionable. You would not believe some of the things I have had students write and mean. I am braced for anything, no matter how ugly or bizarre. If, on the other hand, you are a racist and want to risk it, at least argue your case with a modicum of common sense and logic, not with the kind of inflammatory and emotional nonsense usually associated with the Grand Fleegles of the KKK.

Do not—I repeat, do not—use sarcasm. That way destruction lies. Students, especially those who often use sarcasm in their daily discussions, find they cannot resist sarcastic quips and digs. But these rarely work. In fact, they often backfire. The reason is that sarcasm requires tone of voice to communicate its sarcastic intent. And any tone of voice you might imagine as you write your paper is in your head only and not in the words on the page or in the ears of the reader. You might write, "And of course everybody hates uppity women," intending the comment to be taken sarcastically, but the reader sees only the words on the page, and she may well not read them that way at all. What you hear in a sarcastic voice in your head might well come across as serious intent to an innocent, objective reader. Even Jonathan Swift's "Modest Proposal," an often anthologized example of successful irony in which he urges that abandoned babies be fed to the poor, was taken quite seriously by a horrified few. Communication is difficult enough these days without risking disaster. Most humor, especially satire, depends upon the assumption that your readers share your basic worldview and will therefore recognize a statement wholly outside of that worldview as funny. It is an unfortunate fact of modern American life that there is no longer, if there ever was, a generally accepted worldview. As Ted Danson can confirm, attempts to be funny don't always work. Avoid sarcasm. I always do.

This is particularly true for e-mail. Much of the writing students do these days is on the Internet, where the absence of voice, tone, and facial expression combine with the quickness of response and the shortness of message to create horrendous failures of communication. Many a simple e-mail message has resulted in flame wars that raged on for days until finally burning themselves out. Those cutesy little computer faces, :), technically called "smilies," are a poor substitute for human presence. Anyone who has spent much time on the Internet knows full well the dangers of sarcasm. Do not use it unless you mean it, for someone somewhere will surely take you at your literal word.

Beware also of the flowery and ornate voice, unless you mean to discredit it. I include here not only the baroque rhetorical flourishes of the complete fop but also the attempt to sound more sophisticated than one usually is. Such attempts at erudition can be as hard on the ear as a phony foreign accent. This is perhaps a personal antipathy of my own. But others share it. Much of Mark Twain's *A Connecticut Yankee in King Arthur's Court* is devoted to ridiculing Sir Walter Scott and the idiocies of *Ivanhoe*. Too many students today have spent too much time playing computer variations of Dungeons and Dragons that wallow in the worst sort of a revived, pseudomedieval Sir Walter Scott verbiage. Gag me with a Grue before even thinking of adopting the voice of any of the characters in King's Quest, even if you're a member of SCA.

Closely related is the kind of political BOMFOG that vomits over the airwaves every election season. BOMFOG is a useful acronym for rhetoric that wanders on eloquently about the "Brotherhood of Man and the Fatherhood of God." Such phrases say nothing while trying to give the impression of being vaguely on one side or the other without having to make any specific commitment.

And speaking of commitment, use the active, not the passive, voice. During the Iran-Contra scandal, when the Reagan PR machine finally admitted that "mistakes were made," the *Washington Post* ran an editorial noting the curiously evasive use of the passive voice. Who made those mistakes? The politicians were not going to say. Instead, they withdrew like worms back into the mud of the passive voice.

Dissing the Prof

The main problem with the careful, correct paper is not only that it bores us but that it insults us as well. Try to put yourselves in your English professor's tweed jacket. You are sitting in but one of the prof's three or four courses. In your class alone, 38 papers, each about 5 pages long, have been turned in. That's about 190 mind-numbing pages. If the prof allots, say, 15 minutes to read and correct each paper, that is 570 minutes. Allow 30 minutes here and there to get up, stretch, go to the bathroom, get a beer from the fridge, slop the hogs, and you have 600 minutes of reading, or 10 solid hours. And we are not talking here about a good juicy novel. We are talking about the same thing over and over and over. The repetition is like eternity in a highway traffic jam, inching along, stopping, inching along, stopping. Add to this the fact that most papers written for English classes sound the same—safe, objective, third-person narratives all done in a pseudoscholarly imitation of what students think English professors sound like. And that is where the insult comes in.

Parents of small children are always horrified when they first hear their little darlings sounding just like them. They are supremely embarrassed to see themselves suddenly as others see them. "Oh, my God, is that what I sound like? Good lord, I didn't mean any of that seriously." So too with student papers. By writing in a pseudo–English-professor voice, students are imitating what they think they hear. They are telling us what we sound like to them. I cringe in horror every time. Surely they didn't learn that from me, did they?

Avoid therefore any attempt to sound the way you think an English or history or anthropology paper ought to sound. The results of such efforts are almost invariably pompous and painful. Be true to your own voice, or the voice of your paper, but consider your audience, your readers.

Imagining Your Audience

This is an important rule, not to be brushed over lightly: You must have in mind an idea of who it is you are writing for. And here again, you must fake it. Of course, the reality is that you are writing your college paper for a single reader, the teacher, *moi*. But you must pretend otherwise. I usually tell students to pretend they are writing their English paper for an atomic physicist. This is someone whose intelligence they have to respect but whose knowledge of the latest trends in hip-hop culture may be a bit weak. They therefore have to remind her occasionally of what is going on, but they must do so gently and respectfully without being patronizing or snide. Even the *Washington Post* in publishing a story about golf will gently remind its readers that the foremost celebrity to attend the match was Gerald Ford, "former president of the United States." Chances are that the vast majority of the readers know who Gerald Ford is, but the editors know they still need to remind the occasional absent-minded professor who has been in the lab for the past twelve years.

In the best of all possible possibilities, you should not have an audience in mind at all. You should simply speak from your heart what Emerson calls your "latent conviction." But we have all fallen too far into the labyrinth of constructed voices for that. Lewis Carroll, author of the *Alice* books, offers the best alternative. He was able to write those wonderful little books because he had an audience of one loving, nonjudgmental little girl. He did not worry about her making fun of him, and he knew her well enough to know precisely how to please. Some of the best children's writing, some of the best writing anywhere, is done this way. The first edition of this book was written for only a few students, and I felt free to say it like I felt it. Each edition since then, as it has reached for wider audiences, has, like a presidential candidate leaving the party primaries for the mainstream, gotten just a little less eccentric and less colorful, alas.

Ungrammatical Voices

Here one rule quickly crashes against another. What should you do if you choose to write in a colorful voice but capturing that voice requires writing in ungrammatical English? Can writing according to the strict rules of grammar produce anything but bland, boring prose? *Huckleberry Finn* is a good example of a book written in an ungrammatical voice that in fact succeeds very well despite Huck's lack of formal English. Mark Twain took a risk writing that book, but such risk taking is part of the challenge of writing. Students often complain that I challenge them to be different, to take risks, but that I then give them grief for getting it wrong. And they are right.

A no-person's-land exists between the civilized town and the wilderness. This frontier is where the excitement erupts. No one ever crossed that frontier without the risk of being shot full of arrows by the possessors of that disputed turf. What those students were asking me for were risk-free risks. But good writing takes risks, real ones, and good writers have to get used to that. When you take your pen in hand, or when you load up your word-processor program, you are lighting out for the territory with Huck.

A good example of risky writing would be the use of a distinctive regional voice. To write or to speak correctly all too often means to adopt the standardized WASPy style associated with rural Connecticut or perhaps the Pacific Northwest. The speech patterns of Mississippi, white and black, are practically another language. Do we all have to blend into a bland WASP soup? By no means! Diversity and multiculturalism call us to celebrate the cacophony of voices that make up America. Even if the Mississippi voice is ungrammatical, try it and take the risk.

In one of my composition classes, a disgruntled group of students from the South finally found the nerve one day to rebel against my Bostonian convictions. Not long after insisting that they had graduated "from" high school, not "graduated high school," and that if anything, the high school had graduated them, I had to correct a student for describing someone who was awaiting the arrival of a friend as "waiting on the train." The only person "waiting on a train," I insisted, was the waiter in the dining car. The others were waiting "for" the train. The Southerners fought back, insisting that my wording was as much a regional colloquialism as theirs and that theirs had at least as much legitimacy. I didn't like it, but fearing secession and another Civil War, I conceded the point. After all, people in most of the United States wait "in line," but people in New York wait "on line." In the rest of the country, only AOL users wait "on-line." The Brits "queue up," another good reason for celebrating the Fourth.

That Huck Finn's language was to the ladies of the Concord Library "the veriest trash" demonstrates that some good words do exist over the border of respectability. One such word is "ain't." This much-despised word has done much good work in American letters and does not deserve its uncouth reputation. "It ain't necessarily so" was a great song. "It don't mean a thing/ If it ain't got that swing" is true of writing as well as jazz. Sometimes you have to take a risk. When I was in Slovakia, my departmental chair wrote to tell me that my job had been eliminated. It was a very proper letter, as befits the chairman of an English department, but he could not resist a human touch as well. In parentheses, right after the bad news, he wrote "(ain't I the bearer of good news?)." I showed the letter to my students as a good example of the American ambivalence, the desire for both formal structure and informal personality, liberty and union at the same time. Even the most correct grammarians and language snobs go slumming on occasion. The *New Yorker*, the most exactly edited magazine on earth, once ran an article on a debate that raged at the *New York Times* "with passion and exegetical precision" over the correct spelling of Homer Simpson's favorite expletive. "D'oh" won out over "Duh."

A word I have become quite fond of made front-page headlines in the *Washington Post* when it moved out of the black community and began to echo in the corridors of power. After several young black males got themselves quoted in the paper as having shot people who "dissed" them, this short, sharp substitute for the clumsy "disrespect" gained wide popularity. At first, writers used it in quotation marks to indicate its ambivalent status, but it is now a fairly common word.

Another curiosity is the movement of the word "suck" from clearly obscene to almost acceptable speech. Bart Simpson uses the word on prime time almost any night of the week. But Bart is America's bad boy, our latest incarnation of Huck Finn, and thus is expected to misbehave and use bad English. Recently, the very conservative majority leader of the U.S. Senate, Republican Senator Trent Lott of Mississippi, talking to reporters about a piece of legislation, said, "I told them it sucks but we ought to pass it." The *Washington Post* quoted him verbatim and wrote an editorial suggesting that another s-word, "stinks," might have been a better choice. I agree. "Sucks" was obscene when people hearing it had a picture in their minds of the action it referred to. I suspect neither Bart nor Trent did but threw it out as a pejorative without considering the action the word describes. I prefer language to mean it.

Breezy or Pompous?

The best essays are neither formal expositions in turgid third-person prose nor breezy informal personal stories but a combination of both. Sometimes variety is itself a virtue. One of my favorite writers is the essayist Richard Rodriguez. Part of his charm is that although he is a gay Hispanic Indian who looks like his Aztec ancestors, he has opinions that one would associate with a Boston Brahmin from Beacon Hill. He defies all stereotypes and rejects the expected political clichés. His readers never quite know what to expect. Some hate him for that, but to those with open minds, reading him is a constant surprise and delight. He is also a very good writer. His most anthologized essay, "Aria: A Memoir of a Bilingual Childhood," offers a good example of an argument that moves easily from personal reminiscence to authoritative third-person analysis. He gives a wonderfully moving account of his personal story. But then he steps back from the personal and adopts a more academic voice with which he quotes studies and cites authorities. He moves back and forth between these two modes so gracefully that one hardly notices the transition. More important, he uses the personal voice to establish his understanding of the sentimental argument of those who want to preserve the cohesion of the Spanish-speaking family. In this way, he shows that he understands intimately the arguments of his opponents. Then, in his more formal voice, he explains carefully why, despite the pain, it is important that we all grow up, leave the embrace of the family, and join the wider public community that communicates in English. Here are two voices, a comparison and contrast, and a clear argument and counterargument refuted, definitely an A+ paper.

One of my favorite assignments is to have students write papers describing their favorite food. Even students afraid to open up and brave an opinion find something enthusiastic to say about pizza. These papers are often lively, colorful, and lots of fun. But then, after I assign them a chapter from Marvin Harris's *The Sacred Cow and the Abominable Pig*, a study of the cultural origins of foodways, I have them write a paper exploring the origins of their own personal likes or dislikes. To be done well, this type of paper requires research into psychology, history, anthropology, ethnicity, and ecology. Then, as if that were not enough, I have them combine the two papers trying to retain both the personal enthusiasm of the first paper and the academic analysis of the second. It does not always work. Merging papers after they have been written is harder than writing a varied paper to begin with. But the exercise does get the point across.

5

Plain-Style American Populism

Yankee Doodle's Macaroni

When Yankee Doodle stuck a feather in his cap and called it "macaroni," he was making a statement that was then and remains to this day characteristically American. That feather was as much a text as the Declaration of Independence and as true as the message that underlies this book: that those on the bottom can stick it to the elitists not by getting into Harvard and learning how to play their game but by challenging them in their own vulgar voices.

In the eighteenth-century European courts, "macaroni" was the name of an extremely elaborate Italian hairstyle. Ladies of the court of London, when preparing to attend a ball, would spend hours having their hair done up in huge constructions, often braced by wooden supports that rested on their shoulders. Some would have ships of the line circling around towering beehives. Others would have elaborate birds nesting above. Those stiff minuets that required the head be held high and the back arched had a practical purpose. With his feather, Yankee Doodle is making fun of the aristocrats of England, his cap as much an act of rebellious sarcasm as his name. A "doodle" in eighteenth-century slang was a foolish bumpkin, somewhere between an illiterate redneck and an outright retard. Yankees, of course, were the English settlers of New England. When the Brits sneered at the colonial militia as "Yankee Doodles," they were dissing them something fierce. But rather than hang their heads in shame, these self-reliant Americans, Bart Simpsons to the core, confessed to being Yankee Doodles and proud of it, made a song about it, and used that song to diss the Brits right back.

Here then we get two themes together, the need to accept who we are and not let ourselves be intimidated by the sneers of those who think themselves our betters, and the need to speak back to the elite in our own plain voices.

McMurphy's "Average Asshole"

In Ken Kesey's *One Flew Over the Cuckoo's Nest*, Randle McMurphy finds himself incarcerated in the ward of an insane asylum trying to convince his fellow inmates to stand up for themselves against the bullying of Nurse Ratched. At one point, he shouts at Dale Harding, there to be "cured" of being gay, "Hell, I been surprised how sane you guys all are. As near as I can tell you're not any crazier than the average asshole on the street." With this classic statement of American egalitarianism, McMurphy tears down all of the hierarchical assumptions that make some people feel superior and others inferior. For him the question is not who is sane and who insane in some snooty division of us and them. Instead, his is a planet crowded with different assholes all believing different things and seeing the world in different ways. His let-it-all-hang-out egalitarian attitude is able to accept diversity. He is able to liberate the other inmates from what Martin Luther King called a "psychology of servitude" by showing them not how to conform to society's idea of some political or moral correctness, not how to fit into the prevailing paradigm, but how to ignore society's great shaking finger of shame and, like him, just be themselves.

He is able to do this not because of his superior intellect or his ability to reason and reach logical conclusions; he is able to do this because he has no use or respect for intellect at all. He knows, instinctively, that all of the big words of intellectuals are basically BS, and that at bottom everyone, including himself, is an asshole. Another 1960s icon, the cartoonist Robert Crumb, has a group of black kids confronting an uptight "Whiteman" by telling him, "You jis' a nigger like evva body else. No more, no less, Mutha." This is the beginning of equality.

When Martin Luther attacked the hierarchical assumptions of the Catholic Church and started the Protestant Reformation, he laid the cornerstones of these democratic ideals by insisting that we are not all saints but all sinners. He is quoted as having once said, "The world is an asshole, and I am ripe shit. We are due to be parted soon." No holier-than-thou saint he! Nathaniel Hawthorne used the term "brotherhood of sinners" for this idea that we are all created equal not because we are all potential gods but because we are all equally confused, equally selfish, equally prideful, equally the helpless victims of forces beyond our comprehension and control. An even older phrase for this was "original sin." The American Puritan Jonathan Edwards added an explanation of its significance:

> "This doctrine [of original sin] teaches us to think no worse of others than of ourselves; it teaches us that we are all, as we are by nature, companions in a miserable, helpless, condition; which under a revelation of the divine mercy, tends to promote mutual compassion."

Thus, Harding is never "cured" of being gay. Instead, he stops believing in the combine's put-down of him as somehow inferior or sicker than the "average asshole" and in any more need of a cure than the rest. He learns to reject the put-downs that had convinced him to check into the hospital in the first place. He accepts what once he had viewed as "insanity" as simply another screwed-up way to be. Like Bart Simpson, he is an "underachiever and proud of it."

The line that runs the gamut—from the Puritans' belief in original sin through Jefferson's proclamation that "all men are created equal" to McMurphy's "you're not any crazier than the average asshole out there on the street" to the Bart Simpsons of today's TV—is the democratic ideal that we are all the same under our masks, if not equally gods then equally idiots, but equal nonetheless. This premise may not seem particularly inspiring at first, but you can find here the first step to self-confidence, the realization that even though we may ourselves be less than perfect, no one else, not even the snooty Harvard grad, is any better. Our voices are just as good as theirs, if their voices are just as bad as ours. If all beliefs are equally irrational, contingent, and tied to self-interest, that holds for everyone. "The whole universe," crows Mr. Natural, "is completely insane!" So relax, kid. Even under all your lies and disguises, you are not any worse than the rest of them.

The All-American Con-Man

This acceptance of the reality of our mutual stupidity, as liberating as it is, opens up the terrifying problem of how to know who then to be. What voice should we choose? Our ancestors who left the Old World behind did not want to return, as Scripture says, like a dog to its vomit and carry on the old voices. They came to the wilderness of the New World hoping to be transformed and to be made into new men and women. And in time, they might. But what to do and who to be while waiting? Like any writer facing a blank white page, they found themselves having to fake it.

When Bob Dylan eulogized Allen Ginsberg as "a con-man extraordinaire," he was praising the late, great poet, one American to another acknowledging that which makes us American. Neither the serfs and slaves that we once were, nor the gods we would someday like to become, we find ourselves in the wilderness, Egypt behind us and the Promised Land still far ahead, having to make do as best we can. Not being who we should, we have to construct a persona, put on a mask, and play our parts to the hilt. The lovable con-man, both a con-fidence man and a con-structed man, is one of the great stock figures of American lore. Even after all the king and the duke did to him, when he saw them tarred and feathered, Huck Finn said, "I was sorry for them poor pitiful rascals." Why is that we Americans make such celebrities of actors who play one part after another and seem to have no true personalities themselves? Because, in all too many ways, they are us. Why does Jay Leno get away with telling ethnic jokes? Because, he says, he "degrades everyone equally," and we love it.

Benjamin Franklin is the archetype of the all-American con-man. When he arrived in Paris as our first ambassador during the Revolution, he realized that the French court expected a country bumpkin, so he put on a coonskin cap and conned them all. Then, in his old age, he wrote an autobiography that is one of the great con-jobs of American literature, a model, so Franklin says, for all young people who want to rise in the world. Failing at his effort to construct a perfect persona for himself, he admits, "I cannot boast of much success in acquiring the reality of this virtue, but I had a good deal with regard to the appearance of it."

The day after the Monica Lewinsky scandal broke, Bill Clinton gave a press conference in which he weaved and danced and lied his lies. Finally, one reporter rose and simply asked, "Mr. President, if Monica Lewinsky were here today, what would you say to her?" Caught in midstep, unprepared for the question, Clinton turned, smiled at the reporter, and said, "Oh, that's good. That's real good." A ripple of laughter spread through the room as the reporters all bent forward to see how the con-man extraordinaire would pull it off this time. They knew he knew they knew the game. The entire scandal may have been a shame, but it was also an impressive and successful sham, a truly masterful performance. In the end, the American public sided with Clinton, not because we believed him innocent, but because we identified with the con-man sinner more than we did with the self-righteous, morally perfect, Republican witch-hunters. As Edwards said, a sense of our mutual sinful condition tends to promote mutual compassion. If Clinton could get away with it, so can you.

So choose a voice, put on your mask, march onto the stage of that blank white piece of paper, and construct a story that will wow the crowd.

Empowering or Cowering

Years ago, in a justifiably famous essay titled "Politics and the English Language," George Orwell pointed out that the way politicians use language tends to confuse the public and destroy the clear communication that is the basis of a true democratic politics. His novel *1984* shows how a totalitarian state can destroy people's understanding of the meaning of words in order to keep those people in a state of oppression. The cure for this is for all of us to use words clearly, to insist that academics and politicians speak to us in a language we all can understand. From the days of the Puritans, the plain style has been at the root of all true social revolution. The rules that maintain clear communication are thus tools of progressive, not reactionary, politics. Although some snobs defend strict rules simply to hold onto conservative structures of power, good reasons exist to insist on rules that keep the language from the incomprehensible extremes of both snobs and slobs.

For some reason, academic writers on the left, who, like Orwell, used to be champions of the plain style, today hide themselves in the thick jungle of some of the most impenetrable prose on the planet. This protects them, perhaps, from the state legislators who fund their programs and the parents who pay them to educate their kids. Perhaps the fact that these self-proclaimed radicals sound like the elitists of old is a clue to their true agenda. These would-be party bosses insist that their ideas are so complex that only a complex language can possibly do justice to their subtle brilliance. But when a mischievous scientist named Alan Sokal wrote a satirical piece of nonsense in this style and sent it to a prestigious academic journal, the article was published without a question. Even the practitioners of this style haven't the vaguest idea what it means.

In my own English Department at George Mason University, when the radicals wanted to create a program to push Marxist propaganda under the heading "Cultural Studies," the internal memo describing this new offering had this wonderful defining paragraph:

> Cultural Studies can be understood as the working title for an assemblage of theoretical approaches that are often interdisciplinary and transdisciplinary but also anti-disciplinary. Such work focuses on the analysis and critique of culturally constituted cultural forms and practices and on historically constituted social identities and agencies in the context of their imbrication with the asymmetrical relations of power that permeate the production and reproduction of the economic, political, and ideological dimensions of specific societies.

I love that opening: "can be understood." By whom? The evasive use of the passive voice here is a clue to the passage. What it really says, boiled down to its essence, is that Cultural Studies is a way for academics to explain how rich white guys use their cultural power, as in the writing of books and teaching of grammar, to screw minorities, women, and the poor. If they said that in their application grant to the Republican legislature in Virginia, the chances of this program's getting funded would be rather low. Hence, the use of words like "imbrication" when "overlapping" would have said the same thing. This kind of language does more than puff up the ego of the people who use it; it also obscures their nefarious purposes.

One of my favorite "Shoe" cartoons shows the Perfessor interviewing an eagle from the Pentagon. He asks the eagle, "General, why is it that I can go into any hardware store and buy this wood screw for 2 cents but the Air Force pays $372.17 for the same screw?"

"Very simple," says the general, "You pay 2 cents and you get a wood screw. We in the Air Force pay $372.17, but we get the M-18 fully-slotted, manually activated, fiber-intrusive materials securing unit."

The temptation to read this simply as the posturing of fools needs to be resisted. Far more is at stake. The reason the Air Force pays that much for a screw is because someone is making a profit of $372.15 per screw. That is real money going to a contractor who then pays back his old friends at the Air Force to say nothing of the congressmen who voted for the expenditure.

Voters who are impressed with the pompous language of the Cultural Studies crowd or the inflated descriptions of the Air Force get what they deserve: screwed. Those who insist on the plain style, and who insist that politicians and professors speak in a language we can understand, are the heroes of democracy. Some professors mystically argue that the complex language of Cultural Studies "empowers" students when in fact it belittles them. It makes them feel stupid. True empowerment comes, as Luther and the Reformers knew, when the peasants are taught to read and write in a language they can understand.

Do not therefore be intimidated by complex books. Don't think you have to imitate them. Say it plain and say it proud.

PC Patty

"Crippled" is out, except perhaps when referring to airplanes or the Clinton presidency. Why? Because the word has taken on too much offensive baggage over the years. The word conjures up too many images of sick, diseased, and hopeless human wastes. To call someone crippled is to imply that he or she is somehow inferior. In truth, disabled, handicapped, or crippled people are less able physically, although not mentally or morally. But to admit this is not very nice and allows further unfair insinuations to creep in. So the pressure is on to adopt a value-neutral term, one with no implication of inferiority or inability, a phrase like "differently abled." To use one of the potentially pejorative words is to commit the sin of (I kid you not) "ableism," which is the assumption that able-bodied people are in some ways superior even if that is in fact, in some way, true.

Nor does one avoid this dilemma by avoiding words with negative connotations and using only positive words. After all, one cannot have a positive without a negative. So the use of words with positive connotations, by suggesting that some are better, implies that some must also be inferior. In the academic jargon of the day, even positive language sets up a hierarchy that "privileges" one group over another.

The hope of the PC crowd is that since language influences attitudes, a change in language will create changed attitudes. Forty years of "socialist brotherhood" did little for the Serbs and Bosnians who slaughtered each other from opposite sides of the "Bridge of Unity" after the Red Army left. But hope springs eternal in the American breast. We wish to create utopia even if it means forcing goodness down everybody's sinful throat! Aside from its false assumptions and historical failures, another problem with the plan to change human nature by changing the language is the very real possibility that the old negative connotations will catch up with the new words. Human emotions may well control language as much as language controls human emotions. A cartoon some years back in he *New Yorker* showed graffiti on a hospital wall that read, "Johnny has mental health." A rose by any other name can still draw blood.

Emerson may have said, "Truth is handsomer than the affectation of love," but he was a romantic essentialist. He actually believed there is some absolute truth that can be found or at least felt within the constructed world. But in our confused, relativistic age in which there is no knowable truth, affectation is all we have. So like a Victorian lady, we smile and lie our lies, hoping that somehow the world of words we thus create can replace this dung heap we inherited. Politically correct language is an attempt to deny what once was naively called "truth" in order to create instead a brave new world, a verbal utopia, in which accidental or natural or socially constructed differences no longer exist. If language, after all, is a virtual-reality helmet, then if you don't like this world, unstrap the helmet and try on another. Not that I have anything against niceness, mind you. But when the two values truth and love clash, I prefer the truth, however mean and ugly.

Politically correct language, by substituting "the affectation of love" for truth, would abandon any attempt to break out of these virtual word cages. It would accept the cages of our social constructions as inevitable and turn to the effort to beautify the cages. But some of us are not willing to accept even utopian cultural cages. We would prefer to continue to struggle to take off the helmets, to break out of the cages. We would continue the American Dream of leaving Egypt and risking the dangers of the wilderness in the hope of arriving some day in that promised land of true liberty. Like Huck, we would rather light out for the territory than be civilized. Bitter though it is, people in wheelchairs unable to use their legs are still cripples.

Good writers try to tell what seems to them the truth, and that includes communicating their human value judgments. Writing stripped of all value judgment or opinion is as boring and dry as a legal brief. We may be conditioned and all our values may be virtual and not actual realities, but even then we believe what we believe because we believe it. We can break out of our virtual-reality helmets only by trying to find the cracks in the reality presented, by chasing down what seems to be real until it reveals it-self as virtual or actual. We can get to whatever ultimate truth may exist only by going through the relative beliefs that appear to us as truths. That is why we need to confess the stupidities we as individuals really believe and not pretend to believe in some-body else's constructs. The real danger in permitting the PC po-lice to run rampant is the substitution of someone else's beliefs for our own. No one likes a meddling moralistic Puritan, of the Christian right or the Marxist left, telling us how to live our lives. Like Emerson's rebellious angel Uriel who

> Gave his sentiment divine
> Against the being of a line

we would resist any imposition of a line that is not true to our own (however arbitrarily constructed) voices.

So do try to resist the politically correct pleas for niceness. Tell it straight. Tell your truth, however awkward, embarrassing, or painful. Sin boldly!

Business and Other Jargon

Far be it from me to leave the impression that academics and politicians are the only, or even the worst, abusers of language. Almost every profession feels the need to create its own secret language. Like little boys forming a secret club and speaking only in Openglopish, professionals derive a great sense of secu-rity and status from this game. Sometimes, to be sure, new words (or neologisms, if you must) are needed to communicate new ideas and new technologies. The Internet has provided a flood of such new words with which we have all had to interface. In this way the language grows. But some growth is healthy, and some is cancerous. We English professors try to keep alive the idea that there is a difference, that some but not all new words need to be embraced.

In business, as in the political world, pompous phrases that obscure more than they reveal are particularly loathsome. A quick trip to www.cluetrain.com is highly recommended. You

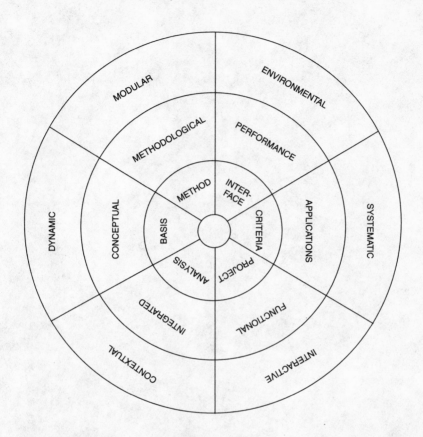

Jargon generator
Spin the dials. Don't stop at three. Pile up as many as you can.

should also study for a moment the Jargon Generator shown here, and imagine spinning either or both of the two outer circles. See how many ways you can create excessive combinations that certainly seem to say something but don't.

Try to remember that the point of writing is communication. If a familiar word will do the trick, use it first. Say "new word" before you say "neologism" and "overlapping" before "imbricating."

6

Choosing Words

Piss and Urine

What is the difference between "piss" and "urine"?

Technically, they are two different words for the same substance. But we all know which is proper and which improper, which to use in polite company or in formal college papers, and which to use in the locker room. Why? Does the fact that doctors prefer "urine" make it acceptable? If so, what caused the doctors or whomever to choose the two-syllable word-sound over the one-syllable word-sound? How do such word choices get made?

The answer is "history."

When William the Conqueror invaded England in 1066, he brought with him a French-speaking aristocracy, imposed on the local Anglo-Saxon population a French ruling class, and created in the process a two-tier social order in which the rulers spoke a Latinate or Romance language and the vulgar peasants spoke their native Anglo-Saxon tongue. Hence, the use of Latin came to signify a member of the aristocracy, and the use of four-letter Anglo-Saxon words came to signify a peasant. In Mark Twain's *A Connecticut Yankee in King Arthur's Court*, Morgan le Fay has a musician executed because he praised her beautiful "red" hair. For persons of a certain social rank, explained Twain, the word for that color is "auburn." By calling her hair "red," the unfortunate musician was implying that Morgan le Fay was an Anglo-Saxon peasant. By putting this distinction in Arthurian England, centuries before the Norman invasion, Twain was committing a horrendous historical anachronism. Nevertheless, the point is a good one for our purposes.

Our language still carries that same political distinction. Four-letter Anglo-Saxon words like "piss" are, literally, vulgar; Latinate words like "urine" are acceptable if not polite. Ezra Pound, the wacko Fascist poet who taught Hemingway how to write, hated the way English toadied to the Latin oppressor. He raged whenever an American writer used a word like "autumn" when the perfectly acceptable Anglo-Saxon "fall" was available.

In England today, in response in part to the French obsession with criminalizing the use of English words like "le weekend," a group called "The Pure English Movement" is trying to eliminate Latinate words from English. These folks want to return to pure Anglo-Saxon words. No "copulation" or "fornication" for them!

The larger point is that our word choices, however unconscious, are loaded with political, social, historical, aesthetic, and moral values that we soak up from our cultural history. Very few words are neutral; almost every syllable we utter has a history and therefore the potential to offend some sensitive soul somewhere. The goal of a value-neutral language is not possible, even if it were desirable, which it is not. We are responsible as writers to be aware of the significance of the words we choose, to know whom we might be offending and why, or why not. Why use this word instead of some other? Why this image or metaphor when a newer one might better make our point?

Think about the words you choose. Avoid wasting words. Intransitive verbs, verbs "to be" and other verbs that simply sit there doing nothing, can almost always be replaced by good, strong, value-loaded action words. Don't say, "The Normans went to England in 1066." Say, the Normans invaded or sailed or conquered or raped or liberated or some other word that adds more information, color, feeling, or opinion to the story. Whenever possible, eliminate "there is" and "it is" from your paper. Replace the pronoun with a noun and the intransitive verb "to be" with an action verb, and be specific. Instead of writing "There was a demonstration on campus yesterday," write "A mob of angry vegetarians destroyed the dean's flower garden in a demonstration against the serving of cooked animal flesh in the campus cafeteria yesterday." Don't choose the first verb or noun that pops into your head. Search for a better one. That is what makes the difference between good and mediocre writers.

Being Niggardly
About the Paddy Wagon

In 1999, a fierce controversy broke out in Washington, D.C., not in the federal but in the predominantly black city government. A white official discussing the budget with two of his black colleagues said the mayor's office had been too "niggardly" with its funding. One of the black officials, convinced he had heard a racial slur, stomped out of the meeting. The white official was promptly fired. The controversy that followed eventually forced the mayor to reinstate the white official, but only after the racist pig had apologized for his insensitive choice of words. To some in the city, it did not matter that the word is of Scandinavian origin and has nothing to do with race. That was a mere technicality. Why did he choose to use a word that sounded like "nigger" when a more familiar "miserly" would have done as well? they asked. Not a bad question. We do need to be careful out there.

On the other hand, we also need to be tolerant. In this, too, our language reflects our society. Words with racist and sexist connotations exist, just as people with racist and sexist attitudes exist. The utopia of universal moral perfection is not around any corners I know of. Jesus may be coming, but he missed another millennium, so until that day does arrive, we must continue changing what we can, tolerating what we can't, and praying for the wisdom to know the difference. Our language is so loaded with historical injustices and unintentional connotations that to cleanse it of sin would be as genocidal as trying to eliminate every sinful American. How many people realize that the term "paddy wagon" comes from the fact that in the nineteenth century, Irish hooligans, or Paddies, were often carted off to jail in them? Is that a slur on the Irish? If you welsh on a bet or get gypped at the mall, should people from Wales and Egypt or the Gypsies get offended? What will my Japanese American nephews, Taiyo and Kenta, do in the fall when there is a nip in the air? How much longer can Italian American children have guinea pigs as pets, listen to doo-wop songs, or order Whoppers at Burger King? Can we ever again say there is a chink in someone's armor? Or go on a Dutch date? Will the Mexican cleaning lady quit if we ask her to mop the floor until it's spic-and-span? I am personally outraged on behalf of all those Asian math students forced by insensitive teachers to compute the slope of the tangent of a curved line.

My point here is not to encourage racist jokes or for that matter to discourage them. Instead, I need to point out, once again, that good writers are conscious writers. They think about the implications of the words they use, and they then choose their words carefully, taking responsibility for whatever might come their way. I salute Senator John McCain, who responded to a complaint about his calling his North Vietnamese prison guards "gooks" by confirming, "That's what those bastards were and that's what I'm going to call them." He knew it was a political risk to talk that way, but he stuck by his words and took his lumps like a man.

The problem that white official in D.C. had was a lack of appreciation for what we call the connotations of language. *Denotation* is what a word literally means; *connotation* is what the word suggests. This of course becomes subtle and depends more on the reader or the listener than the writer. But a good writer uses the connotations of language to imply and insinuate. To call a female dog a "bitch" may be technically correct, but it isn't innocent. Words can hide their true impact behind literal facades. Sometimes, the mind unconsciously reacts to a word in an altogether different way from that assumed by the innocently literal mind. Sexually suggestive language can, innocently or not, be sprinkled throughout even the driest legal brief without either the lawyer or his client realizing why they are both getting so charged. Sometimes advertisers smuggle in such subliminal messages.

I have always wondered about Popeyes Chicken. Why is it called "Popeyes"? The famous cartoon character is not part of the advertising, and the one food item Popeye was famous for, spinach, is not even on the menu at Popeyes. And shouldn't there be an apostrophe before the s?

But when I learned that the founder of Popeyes was a devout Catholic from Louisiana, a state so Catholic that the counties are called parishes, I looked again and saw in the seemingly innocent name the evidence of a fiendish papist conspiracy, the likes of which have not been seen since the Gunpowder Plot of 1605. You may not have noticed consciously, but your subconscious may have taken in how the middle "e" slants slightly to the right and the "y" slightly to the left dividing the name into the two words "Pope yes." Is the popularity of the current Polish pope perhaps the result of this subliminal advertising campaign? When the Vatican's Swiss guards sail up the Potomac, seize the White House, and are welcomed enthusiastically by drumstick-waving converts, remember you read it here first.

Snobs and Slobs

We have, and have always had, in American English a classic battle between conservatives on one side who are afraid the structures that provide our security are in danger of collapse, and radicals on the other who seem willing to embrace any new fad that promises utopia. The conservatives want to retain the rules of grammar and diction and punctuation as handed down to them by their grandfathers. If it was good enough for Jesus, then it's good enough for them. Any change appears to them like the Hun at the gate about to pillage the city. These language snobs can be found in the letters-to-the-editor pages of all our major newspapers bewailing the fate of the republic if people don't follow every jot and tittle of the classic rules.

The position of the radicals, on the other hand, can be illustrated by the argument of a book that came out in the 1970s, before anyone had every heard of ebonics, called *The Way It Spozed to Be*. The argument there, as in the more recent *Yo Mama's Dysfunktional!* was that the rules of language reflect the reality of human speech and that we ought not try to standardize the speech patterns of minority communities but instead allow minority languages an equal legitimacy with so-called standard English. Such language slobs would have us simply go with the flow, carried along on the flood of popular culture wherever that may lead, into whatever balkanized anarchy.

The wonderful thing about this debate is that both sides are right. We need a common set of rules if we are to communicate effectively. We do need structure. But we also need the freedom to break from those rules when they oppress our creative instincts. America itself is a product of this dispute, constantly torn between its existence as a "unum," one nation indivisible, and a "pluribus," 270 million of us each doing his or her own thing. Just before the Civil War, Daniel Webster defended the Union with the cry, "Liberty and Union! Now and Forever!" The Southerners listening replied that if the North kept its Union, they were being denied their liberty. The Northerners responded that the South's liberties seemed to include the liberty to enslave others. Contradictions abound. It may be an impossible dream, but we Americans all still cherish the ideal of having both liberty and union, pluribus and unum, freedom and structure, now and forever. Let lesser nations be forced to choose. In this land of plenty, we'll take both.

In fact, we Americans already are mostly a nation of happy slobs and proud of it, preferring when the conflicts come the chaos of liberty over the security of structure, Bill Clinton over some fundamentalist pope. People of other nations, like the French, have official bodies that guard the purity of the national language and pass laws governing what can be said and written in public. In the United States, we cross our fingers and trust freedom. But as with the arguments over gun control, abortion, and the legalization of pot, some demand stricter control, and some trumpet the freedoms of the Bill of Rights. Traditionally, English professors are expected to be more snob than slob, but lately the politics of academia has been on the side of an open-ended diversity. Grammar, we are told, is a plot to privilege the distinctive language style of white male WASPs and thus perpetuate the political dominance of that cultural class. Hence the teaching of grammar on my campus is considered politically incorrect. I do it, but I close the doors and whisper.

Even this book, then, is a political act, and the words I choose mark me. You thus need to think carefully before you choose your words. You need to be aware of the language battle raging around you. Only then can you choose consciously, and with full knowledge of the consequences, how much of a snob or how much of a slob you want to be. Worse yet, that this is an ongoing war between two eternal factions means you have no generally accepted rule you can safely follow. Some teachers are more snob; some more slob. Which you are going to be is up to you, not some authority.

Along with this debate goes the perennial pedagogical punch-out between those snobs who insist that students master the traditional rules of grammar and those slobs who think it more important to empower students by allowing their oppressed voices to burst out of the shackles of patriarchal rules. The snobs argue that learning how to write correctly is a tool that empowers students, that students who master the "correct" way to write can get good jobs, seize control of their lives, and escape from whatever ethnic or class ghettos entrap them.

The slobs respond that "correct" means "by the standards established by white males in order to make everyone else play by the rules of which they are already the masters." They argue that it is more important that students be allowed to express themselves in their own idioms and styles and punctuation and not be made to feel illiterate and stupid simply because they are different. This, the slobs say, truly empowers students by allowing them the freedom of their subcultures.

My view is that both standard grammar and the liberation of individual voices are needed. Just as a good jazz musician must first master the scales and fingering of his of her instrument, so the writer must, as the snobs insist, master the technicalities of grammar. But just as technical mastery alone cannot a jazz master make, so a writer must also learn how to dig down and release his or her individual soul before the music can swing. Expression without form is the wailing of an infant, but form without all that primal energy is as dead as the letter without the spirit. We need both.

Clichés

Avoid these like the plague.

Now, when was the last time you personally had to avoid bubonic plague? Not recently, I'll bet. This is a good example of a cliché, a phrase with no immediacy, no life, merely a collection of words left over from some other time repeated to the point that people pay no attention to what the words say. We get the idea; that's about it.

Emerson had the best lines on this problem. Language, he said, is fossil poetry. In its youth, it is fresh and alive and creates vibrant pictures. But in time phrases become fossilized abstractions, no longer able to conjure up images of anything real. It is the writer's job, indeed the prophet's job, to reconnect words to living things, to create new images that come alive in the mind and ear. Corrupt men with dead souls simply repeat stale phrases. Like Senator Trent Lott, they use the word "suck" without bothering to let a picture form in their minds. "But wise men," says Emerson, "pierce this rotten diction and fasten words again to visible things; so that picturesque language is at once a commanding certificate that he who employs it is a man in alliance with truth and God."

All language is metaphor, and it is up to us to keep the mind alive by keeping the metaphors of language alive. We should always be looking for new ways to say old truths. The first person who said, "It ain't over till the fat lady sings" was a poet. That picture was so true and so to the point that the phrase was repeated many times over. Within a year it was already a cliché. On election day 1992, a group of large ladies gathered at the White House gates to serenade George Bush, momentarily resurrecting the cliché and attesting to the power of a common language of shared imagery. Today, we are witnessing the evolution of several computer terms from fresh expression through cliché into ordinary language in what may be record time. Once it took generations for phrases to become clichés; today, thanks to the mass media, a good phrase can be destroyed in a nanosecond. "Information highway" was the phrase that emerged to describe the Internet, e-mail, and all their associated peripherals. Some thought "town dump" was a better metaphor. After all, users of the Internet search through piles of garbage for the few bits of treasure, and yet, as an older saying had it, one man's trash is another's treasure. "Information highway" quickly became such an overused phrase that it developed the stale smell of a cliché. Today, the term is already beyond the cliché stage and so standard a word that most writers no longer cringe when they hear it. Apparently, as space expands, time speeds up, and down we hurtle ever faster through the cosmos.

Such phrases, after excessive use, no longer evoke pictures but become ordinary words with no vestige left that they were once poetry at all. The word "nitpicking" is my favorite example. We all know what it means; it means to go at some task in tiny and painstaking detail. "Nitpicking" is itself a word for a general concept. But what picture does the phrase depict? What is a nit, and why is it being picked? A nit is the egg case of a crab louse. In the bad old days before the availability of such products as Kwell, mothers in America had to sit down with their children and examine their heads for lice. After killing as many lice as they could find, they faced the task of sliding the sticky nits off the child's hair one at a time, strand by strand, or of pulling out the individual hairs that had these tiny nits stuck to them. It was a tedious job, and our nineteenth-century ancestors had a vivid picture in their minds when they heard the term "nitpicking." Today, it is merely another word. Where is the poet who will create a new word or phrase that depicts this idea with an image true to our modern experience? Perhaps some literate computer nerd like my son Nathan will come up with the perfect phrase for a job that involves millions of tiny chores and painstaking attention to detail.

Emerson and I and English teachers everywhere await that day. We reward the student who has a fresh ear for words in new combinations. In the meantime, we point out clichés whenever we recognize them, hoping against hope that some student someday will get the idea and produce the brilliant poetry that will, inevitably, become a cliché of the future.

This is what poets try to do. Some fail, but the successful ones create fresh images that stick in the mind. Camille Paglia, the

wild woman of academia, has a way of using language like Joan
of Arc swinging a bloody sword. After explaining her theory that
Apollonian males, in flight from nature, need culture to protect
their all-too-exposed natural parts, whereas women, with their
important body parts internalized, are more secure but have less
reason to be culturally creative, she creates a picture that cap-
tures this notion. Stated in the abstract, this is provocative
enough, but the impact of this abstract language cannot compare to the shock of the image she uses to illustrate her point:
"Male urination really is a kind of accomplishment, an arc of
transcendence. A woman merely waters the ground she squats
on." Whatever one makes of her theories, no one can deny that
Ms. Paglia is a good writer. She keeps her readers alert.

Ezra Pound told his students to learn new languages to liberate themselves from the idioms and clichés of English. Try Ara-
bic or Gaelic, he told Archibald MacLeish, when MacLeish
confessed his inability to escape from clichés. In a letter to his
friend Ernest Hemingway, MacLeish complained that Pound
"was as full of shit as a cesspool. What's wrong with clichés anyway? Why should we let ourselves be chased up into the ravines
just because the good soil had already been farmed before us?"

It was a fair question. And MacLeish had a point. Since all language is "fossil poetry," almost every phrase is a cliché. We cannot write every phrase entirely anew or we'll end up as
incomprehensible as Gertrude Stein. But that is no excuse for
wallowing in the worst of the cesspool. We can strain against
fate and fight against habit and, who knows, maybe even create
some new phrases in the process. To leave as a legacy a new
phrase or word is to have expanded the collective consciousness
and to have more than justified one's existence. Good writers are
the heroes who free us from the tyrannies of clichés and open up
the future.

Language, after all, reflects and further shapes our lives. If we
write in clichés, we will think in clichés, never leaving the paradigms of our youth. We all have clichés, or paradigms, that have
shaped how we read the world. How many baby boomers see
every confrontation between blacks and whites as if it were still
1963 with every black man another Martin Luther King and

every white cop Bull Connor? How many Republicans see every
proposed reform as an excuse for some fat labor boss to steal
their money? Many Americans trapped in the clichés of the past
still think that any black man accused of mugging a little old lady
for her welfare check must be guilty. In a similar way, when
Tawana Brawley said she had been abused by white cops, many
liberal Americans, faithful to the 1960s paradigm, never doubted
she was telling the truth. We all, left and right, black and white,
need to move off the 'digm and think in new ways, without
clichés.

Say What You Mean—
Mean What You Say

Pay attention to what you are literally saying. Pay attention to
what your words mean, not just what you intend them to mean.
Students come to me constantly with their graded papers in
hand whining, "Well, what I meant to say was . . ." or "But you
know what I meant to say." Sorry, it is your job to mean what
you say and to say what you mean, and it is my job to play the innocent, unsuspecting reader. I must respond to what I read on
the page; my task is not to give you the benefit of the doubt and
not to read into your confused words what I want you to mean.
Don't say "Literally climbing the walls" unless you are writing
about Spiderman. If you mean figuratively, say so. The bottom
line in almost all of this is don't pop off with the first thing that
comes into your head, but think about your words before you
write them.

A close relative of the cliché, the mixed metaphor is another
example of how we use phrases without paying any attention to
the picture conjured up by the words. The classic Western Civ
101 mixed metaphor has Dante "standing with one foot in the
medieval world while with the other he saluted the rising dawn
of the Renaissance."

A published article I use in my composition class refers to
women's "underground struggle" for equality. The phrase has a
compelling nobility, and I suspect the author used it because it
"felt right." But had she thought about it after feeling it, she

might have asked whether in fact the women's rights movement in America was ever an "underground" movement. The Seneca Falls convention of 1848 was certainly aboveground and covered in the press of the day. When the suffragettes marched up Pennsylvania Avenue and chained themselves to the White House fence in the teens, they were hardly hiding underground. If anything, the women's rights movement has been marked by its open and public character right from the start. This is a good example of the use of a word for its vague emotional appeal, its connotation, and not because of its literal meaning. Poets might get away with this sort of sloppiness, but writers of prose should know better.

Here we face that vague no-person's-land between the realm of emotion and the realm of rational thought. I would be the last person to deny that our rational thoughts are tied to their emotional sources. Writing cannot exist in some mythical rational realm above emotion. The notion that these are two entirely separate phenomena and that thought can occur without emotional entanglement is positivist nonsense. Nevertheless, people say and write "feel" far too often when in fact they mean "think." If your girlfriend comes in wearing a stunning blue dress, you would not say, "I feel that dress is blue." You might, however, say, "I feel stunned by the beauty of that blue dress." The use of "feel" over "think" is fueled by our increasingly democratic society in which personal feelings are beyond reproach. We can criticize people for their thoughts, since thoughts are somehow seen as being less personal, but feelings are akin to religion. Each person is entitled to his or her own. Nevertheless, as democratic and nonjudgmental as we may want to be, good reasons remain for retaining the distinction between feeling and thinking. I am braced for the day some student in math class says, "I feel that one and one is three" and no one dares to question his feeling.

Another pet peeve of mine is the current popularity of the word "sensitivity." We must be sensitive to minority concerns, to women's concerns, to the problems of disadvantaged persons of all types. And yet what does the word "sensitive" mean? Does the racist bigot who uses subtly coded phrases to belittle the

African Americans in her class lack sensitivity? If she were not sensitive to the pain her words caused, how could she know exactly where to stick in the pins? One can be both sensitive and racist. On the other hand, if a racist student is causing tension in the class, shouldn't the teacher confront that student in a way that must necessarily offend her? Doesn't it take a fair degree of insensitivity to confront that student and make her shut up? Or should a sensitive teacher understand the depths of pain out of which that racism comes and avoid hurting the poor girl's feelings? The people who use this term seem to mean not emotional sensitivity but sensitivity to their personal political positions. They carefully pick and choose those whom they want to be sensitive to and those whom they want to offend. This seems somewhat dishonest, as if they could push their politics not on the basis of political or ideological merit but on the basis of feeling. It is a left-wing equivalent of the conservative attempt to inflate particular political stands to the stature of patriotism or godliness and thereby avoid having to debate the issue. Let us puncture all such phony language.

Eugene Genovese, the eminent historian, has argued that when he was in college in New York City, the classroom was an ideological war zone in which professors acted as if they were paid "to assault their students' sensibilities, to offend their most cherished values." In that way, students learned to defend themselves with argument, analysis, and evidence. This style of learning is perhaps too narrowly grounded coming as it does out of a Talmudic tradition of argument and confrontation as a way of getting to the truth. But Genovese continues to use it to advantage and argues, "I know no other way to show students, black or white, male or female, the respect that ought to be shown in a place of ideological and intellectual contention." I applaud and submit to you, then, Genovese's first law of college teaching:

> Any professor who, subject to the restraint of common sense and common decency, does not seize every opportunity to offend the sensibilities of his students is insulting and cheating them, and is no college professor at all.

Sexist Language

Should student writers today stick to the traditional use of "he" and "man" to refer to people in general, or should students go along with the current crusade to eliminate gendered language? Well, if that writer wants to pass his or her course, given the political climate in academia today, he or she had better knuckle under fast. Only the fuddiest duddies still defend masculine pronouns as being somehow universal. The rest of us recognize the not-so-subtle implications of using the masculine pronoun to mean "people." File this one under the category of saying what you mean and meaning what you say. "He" means a man, and "she" means a woman. Use them that way.

The feminist crusade to reshape the language stems from the fact, already noted, that seemingly innocent word choices are loaded with political and social implications. A politically neutral language, if one could imagine such a thing, would be as worthless as a politically neutral politician. We want our words to be taking risks and saying something. What we want is not a value-free language but a language of balanced interest groups, not a bland gray but a riotous mosaic of color. For years the baby doctor Benjamin Spock referred to the baby as "he" and "him." In his last edition of *Baby and Child Care*, he tried to atone for a lifetime of error by referring to the baby as "she." In the 1970s, a brief movement arose to create the gender-neutral "shem" to replace "him" when that pronoun is used to mean "people." A move was also begun to replace Mrs. and Miss with Ms. Despite the long refusal of the *New York Times* to go along, "Ms." has become an accepted part of the language; "shem" never got off the ground.

In this book, you will undoubtedly notice that I use a bit of every alternative. At times I use "him" and assume the masculine; at other times I use "her" and assume the feminine. Occasionally I use the clumsy "his and her" and include both. Since writing ought to reflect real speech, "his/her" and "he/she" are unacceptable. Nobody says "his/her," so nobody ought to write it. In divinity school, where the gender war was waged with an unholy fierceness, I once solved the difficult problem of which pronoun to use in reference to the deity by writing "s/he/it." The professor was not amused.

The best solution to the gender dilemma is to leap into the plural, something only polytheists can do when referring to God. There English provides us with the grammatically acceptable and gender-neutral "them" and "they." Thus, "A student must bring his (or his and her, or his/her) books" can become "All students must bring their books." Rewriting your sentence so that the plural pronoun can be used may save you from the wrath of the grader.

Past and Present

Write about texts in the present tense; write about events that occurred in the past in the past tense. In what we call the "historical present," the book is alive even if the author is dead. Therefore, in *Moby Dick*, Captain Ahab says, "That inscrutable thing is chiefly what I hate; and be the White Whale agent, or be the White Whale principal, I will wreak that hate upon him." But Herman Melville wrote those words in 1850. Ahab lives on, but Melville, the author, is history. Note that Melville's voice in the text, like Ahab, lives on. Melville "wrote" the book, but in the book Melville "says." If you remember that books are considered to be alive, you should have no problem.

When using different tenses, do be careful. If you are writing in the past tense and you refer back to an event that occurred even earlier, be sure to use the pluperfect "had." When you return to the past time in which you started, be sure to return to the past tense. One way to remain clear and to avoid confusing your readers is to keep each tense consistent within a paragraph and not bounce back and forth between different time zones in any one paragraph. Keeping your tense straight will go a long way toward helping keep your reader straight. Remember where you are and when you are.

Poetic Prose

In choosing words, be sure to listen to the rhythm of your language. English likes to gallop along at a steady pace, half a league, half a league, half a league onward, into the valley of A's, wrote the best word bard. You do not have to count stressed syllables.

Either you have an ear for rhythm or you don't. If you do, listen to it. If you don't, listen to music or children's poetry. I grew up on A. A. Milne's wonderful poems in *When We Were Very Young*. To this day I can still recite all the stanzas of

> James James
> Morrison Morrison
> Weatherby George Dupree
> Took great
> Care of his Mother,
> Though he was only three.
> James James
> Said to his Mother,
> "Mother," he said, said he:
> "You must never go down to the end of the town,
> if you don't go down with me."

Moby Dick is a great book for many reasons, but one of them is the sheer poetry of Melville's prose. Hundreds of people get together in New Bedford every year and read it aloud just for the joy of hearing the words. In my own editing, I have often felt that a phrase "just wasn't right" only to discover that the reversal of a word or two restored a rhythm I had not even known was there.

You may even have noticed by now that I am addicted to alliteration. Some think it a curse, but they are, as William Safire once wrote, "nattering nabobs of negativism." Just as the ear likes to hear the first part of any paper echoed at the end, so the ear likes to hear rhythm and internal rhyme. At least mine does, and I suspect most English teachers are English teachers because they love the sounds of English. Even some of the dogmatists who have tried to turn departments of English into political-propaganda factories have renounced their heresy and returned to the love of words for their own sake. Don't be afraid to sing.

7

Arguing Your Case

No Right or Wrong

When I first boarded that tramp steamer right out of high school, I was as sick as vomit for several weeks, but I had to work anyhow between trips to the leeward railing. I would often glance out the porthole while I was mopping below decks and wish I could be as fixed and steady as the horizon. One day, after the seasickness had subsided, I glanced out the same porthole and was startled to discover not the ship but the horizon slowly tilting back and forth. What had happened, without my knowing it, was that I had adjusted to the center of gravity of the freighter and no longer was trying to stand in relation to the center of gravity of the earth. I had broken my allegiance with the globe and tossed my fortunes in with 8,000 tons of rolling steel. Which was the true center of gravity? Is there one? When we fly into space and leave the earth behind, are we climbing or falling? If two rocks pass each other in space, can we tell if both are moving at half the relative speed, or if either one alone is doing all the moving? Science tells us that the earth circles around the sun and the moon around the earth, but if either the earth or the moon could be held still in space, wouldn't the cosmos continue to dance around them as the fixed points just the same? It is all relative. It all depends, as Clinton said, on what the meaning of "is" is. There well may be a Truth out there. I believe there is. But that does not give me, or anyone, access to it. Even Scripture was translated, and the translation still needs to be interpreted.

So once again, it bears repeating, don't worry about being "wrong." Being wrong is, at least in the humanities, almost impossible because there are no "right" answers. The academic journals are filled with new and bizarre interpretations of old favorites, and the more bizarre the theory, the more likely it is to get published and to win some clown tenure and a lifetime job grading sophomore papers. What we teachers mean with a D grade is that we find no real argument or that the argument is illogical or is not supported by evidence or perhaps is inconsistent with other evidence in the text. Sometimes it means we cannot be sure you read the right book. The English teacher who asks, "What is the meaning of this poem?" is a fool. There is no one "the meaning." There are interpretations, and there are arguments for those interpretations. That is all we really know. People who insist they really know what they are doing are fooling themselves or you or both. Only the saints who have heard directly from God know the Truth; the rest of us are stuck in the constructed dung heaps of the earth.

Poets themselves love to confess to being "inspired" *ab extra*, from outside themselves. "I is another," said Arthur Rimbaud. "Sing in me, muse," sang Homer, "and through me tell the story." Certain words or images were put in poems because they "felt right," but the poets often are no more certain why than we readers are. They know what they thought they were doing, but something else may have been going on of which they were totally unaware.

No intelligent person can deny the conditional or contingent nature of consciousness. We are shaped by unconscious forces in the environment and the soul. Sometimes it is easier for a stranger to see through our best rationalizations and expose us even to ourselves. So do not fall into the trap of imagining that some hidden "right" answer exists on which all the experts secretly agree. Received opinion is often wrong and usually boring; the text is yours to interpret. It certainly helps to show that you know and understand the conventional wisdom or the professor's pet theory, but do not be afraid to go beyond it. This is as true for the social sciences; if you don't like the standard Marxist or psychological or feminist analysis, try another or try your own.

Imagine Jesse Jackson, Jesse Helms, and Jesse Ventura each writing a history of the Clinton presidency. All three texts will be histories. But which one is "right" would be very much a matter of subjective political perception. Some reviewers will judge the books entirely on the basis of their own prejudices, of course disguising their bias under the illusion of objectivity. Liberals will hail the Jackson history as "inspired," "insightful," and "eloquent" while condemning the Helms history for its narrow ethnocentricity. Conservatives will praise the Helms history for its "penetrating analysis" and "constructive moral perspective" while condemning the Jackson history for being unscholarly and unobjective. *Playboy* will run excerpts of the Ventura history. All the reviewers will find objective reasons for their subjective opinions, and it is on these that disinterested readers (if there are any) will have to make their judgments. Thus, each reviewer will try to find fault with the logic, with the evidence, and with the perspective of the text while searching out reasons for praising the text the reviewer is biased toward. As Melville showed us in his chapter on the "Doubloon," we see ourselves in the text. A recent scholarly biographer of Ronald Reagan wrote himself into the biography even though he hadn't been born when the events described occurred. In doing so, he may have been more honest than those biographers who think they are being objective. As that cynic Pontius Pilate so succinctly put it, "What is truth?" We call this scholarship.

Histories written about the dynasties of the kings of England are no different from histories of the dynasty of Bill and Hillary. The older histories seem more objective only because we are no longer party to the passions and debates that shaped the different viewpoints of their politics. But just as we can find a dozen different angles from which to analyze any political event today, so too can we find dozens of ways in which to look at any historical or psychological or theological or literary event of the past. Even worse, we have to multiply the number of different parties competing by the number of different lenses through which we can interpret their disputes today. That is why we say in the humanities that there are no right answers, only opinions and arguments in favor of those opinions. Hence, you cannot be wrong in terms of your argument. You can only be judged fairly on the basis of how you argue, how you use evidence, cite sources, draw conclusions, and refute your critics.

Therefore, the bolder the argument, the better the chance the paper will score well. We teachers are not expecting you to discover some specific buried message or "deeper meaning" hidden cleverly in the text. We expect you to come up with any interpretation that takes the literal meaning of the text into account and also finds something of interest that is not immediately obvious. Be logical, be informed, be opinionated, back up your points with a lot of facts, evidence, and quotations, and bring in some outside artillery. You can't lose. Only the most bigoted fool of a teacher will nuke you for daring to be different. Such teachers do exist, but they are rarer than you think, and you can go to them and explain that you are really not the crypto-Nazi skinhead whose voice you were assuming (faking, remember?) in your paper. Note that a certain degree of sensitivity to the sensitivities of us sometimes all-too-sensitive teachers is wise policy.

Battle Tactics

Imagine an argument as a military maneuver. Once you state your objective in the topic paragraph, you need to begin to move your troops forward. But before you can make your first move, you must consider your tactics. These will depend largely on your objective and on your opponents. Are you trying to persuade people who already disagree with you? If so, that will require confrontation and refutation. Are you trying to persuade a neutral audience? If so, then you want to be careful not to confront them or you might lose the possibility of winning them over. Much of this depends on the voice you choose and the assumptions you make.

Many arguments fail because the writer makes unwarranted assumptions. If you wish to prove that evolution is a false theory, appeals to the Bible or quotations from fundamentalist ministers might not succeed. You personally might be persuaded by such arguments, but unless your opponent already agrees with you that the Bible is always literally true, you will be resting your argument on an unwarranted assumption, and you will not convince a soul. To avoid this problem, you must either find a common assumption you can work from, or you must first persuade the reader that the Bible is in fact true. Good luck.

Finding a common ground is a good way to begin your argument. If you can establish a common basis upon which you and your readers agree, then you have a solid base from which to build a persuasive case. We Americans tend to believe that anything "natural" is good. Thus, analogies from nature are common rhetorical devices. Both feminists and male chauvinists appeal to nature to back up their arguments about the proper relationship between the sexes in human society. In the New Testament, Jesus was very fond of analogies, repeatedly comparing difficult concepts to familiar ones: "And why take ye thought for raiment? Consider the lilies of the field how they grow; they toil not, neither do they spin: Yet I say unto you that even Solomon in all his glory was not arrayed like one of these."

Such analogies can be very persuasive, but they can also be very misleading. Before the 1960s, arguments in favor of segregation of the races were often based upon analogies with nature: Birds of a feather flock together, don't they? Thus, one needs to consider the assumptions being made even here. Nature isn't always friendly. Analogies to what we already understand and believe can be very seductive, but they can also be deceptive. Use them, but think them through carefully.

Arguments that begin with some common assumption or an analogy with some generally accepted truth are called "inductive." An inductive argument begins with some general statement that leads to certain specific conclusions. If the reader agrees with the assumption, the argument should prove successful. But in our pluralistic, fragmented world, there are few, if any, common assumptions left that very many people agree on. And most teachers, if they are any good, can shoot any unproven assumption full of holes. Thus, inductive arguments tend to be less successful than deductive arguments. These are arguments that begin with specifics, with evidence, and then draw general conclusions from that specific evidence.

Be prepared, therefore, once you have stated the point you want to establish, to be able to present evidence to back up your claim. The more evidence you can bring up to the front, and the greater variety of evidence you can muster, the better your chance will be of carrying the field. Begin with a proposition or a question or a challenge. Define any potentially questionable terms you might need to use. Then bring in the evidence with which to prove your point. Do not assume that a mere stating of the case is sufficient. Evidence that seems clear to you may seem irrelevant to your reader. You must explain logically how that evidence supports your claim.

This evidence must also be made up of facts, not opinion. We define facts as statements that can be verified by outside observers. Even this is subjective, of course. The *Washington Post* requires three independent verifications before it declares a statement to be a fact; the *New York Times* requires five. You may believe that Jesus rose from the dead, but it is not a fact unless it can be proved by outside evidence. Quotations from the Bible, the book in which this claim is made, cannot be considered as outside evidence.

Another way to think of your argument is to imagine that you are Johnny Cochran arguing his case before a jury. First you have to have a case to argue. You need to let the jury know where you are headed. You need to keep them awake and paying attention. You need to present the facts and the evidence in a logical manner using language they can understand. You need to make sure they understand how that evidence fits into your overall argument. You need to refute the argument of the prosecuting attorney. And you need to sum up your case at the end with a bang so that the jurors will be impressed. You might even use a little poetry. If it doesn't fit, they must acquit!

VGs, AEs, and OAs

Many years ago, the *Harvard Crimson* published a guide by a successful student who had mastered the art of passing an exam without studying. "Beating the System," as the essay was called, listed three basic approaches to writing exam essays: the Vague Generality (VG), the Artful Equivocation (AE), and the Overpowering Assumption (OA).

The VG is an easy trap to fall into, but it is to be avoided at all costs. Papers full of VGs are raging seas of confused winds and currents in which the seasick reader prays that the ship will hit a solid rock and bring all the nauseating dizziness to an end. VG papers have no facts, no solid opinions; they paint no pictures. They are hot, stagnant dinosaur breath. A wonderful "Doonesbury" cartoon depicts Mike entering a room where Zonker is writing a term paper. It is full of vague generalities and indirect allusions and BS: "Most problems, like answers, have finite resolutions. The basis for these resolutions contain [*sic*] many of the ambiguities which conditional man daily struggles with. Accordingly, most problematic solutions are fallible." Mike asks, "Which paper is this?" Responds Zonker, "Dunno. I haven't decided yet." Zonker's essay is a good example of a string of VGs. They have no substance, no meat, no facts, and they immediately send a signal to the reader that the writer hasn't a clue. (Note also my *sic* highlighting Zonker's noun-verb agreement problem; Zonker hadn't read *Sin Boldly!*)

The Artful Equivocation is a little better, but not much. It at least gives the student who hasn't the vaguest idea of the answer the opportunity to show what he or she does know. An AE essay usually is full of waffles: "Whether one defines Shelley as a Romantic depends upon a host of complex variables." An essay on the causes of the Great Depression by someone who didn't get that far in the text might begin, "Before one can hope to understand the causes of the Depression of the 1930s, it is necessary to understand as fully as possible the social conditions of the decade that preceded it." The student can then write about bathtub gin and flappers, at least giving the grader something to grade, even if it is not the desired answer. AE essays often give themselves away with the use of that all-purpose inanity adopted by TV anchors, "remains to be seen."

The Overpowering Assumption, however, is the best approach. The OA is the equivalent of Luther's "sin boldly." It is simply the assumption of an opinion so bold and imaginative, if totally off the wall, that the reader will be impressed by the sheer daring involved: "The American Civil War was caused not by slavery or the economics of cotton, but by the North's fear that Southern aristocrats would spread their oppressive institutions into the North and kill the American experiment in freedom." A few facts and a little logic thrown in to back up the OA are all that is needed. Don't worry too much about being "right." Make the best argument you can for the assumption you are pushing. Be bold.

When I was teaching in Czechoslovakia, I was confronted with papers by students who had learned the careful art of saying nothing, and learned it well. Life under communism had taught them to avoid committing themselves to any ideas, even Marxist ones. They never knew when even the party line might swerve and leave them stranded. So their papers were masterpieces of vague generalities and artful equivocations: "In certain situations, certain events can cause certain repercussions. In such circumstances, it is always best to choose the best solution to the given problems." Zonker had nothing on these kids. But you don't have communism as an excuse for hiding, and neither do they anymore. Still, sometimes bad habits left over from the tyrannies of our youth maintain their grip on our souls. We must fight against them. We must be bold.

Show What You Know and Define Your Terms

If I ask a class of students if they believe in God, several brave souls will raise their hands. If I ask if they do not believe, another few hands go up. The rest will admit to being skeptics or agnostics. But if I ask the same students if they believe in skartz-dreg, most will look puzzled and ask what the word means. They should have asked the same question of that other word, "God." Why didn't they? Because they assumed that they knew and that I knew what they knew, both assumptions utterly wrong. Defining the terms of the debate is often the whole of the debate. More often than not, people fight not because they disagree but because they do not realize what the other side is saying. It is important, therefore, to define your terms and to be sure the reader knows what you are talking about.

Knowing that they are in fact writing for an audience of one, their teacher, some students are tempted to omit important points or to slide glibly over them with an "as you know," knowing full well that I do know because I taught the course. The problem here is that the purpose of the paper is to help me find out if you know. Therefore, no matter how obvious and repetitious it may seem, you do need to show that you know the basic facts and ideas and definitions. If you repeat a word you heard used several times in class, a generous professor may give you the benefit of the doubt and say, "Well, this student must understand this term in order to have used it." Not me. I have read enough papers by students trying to cover up the fact that they don't even know the title, author, or main character of the book we've been carefully studying for two weeks. Such experiences have made me quite cynical. Show me.

In the development of the paper, you will undoubtedly be using some general terms. These need to be defined. Freedom? Democracy? Racism? Romanticism? Marxism? Structuralism? You may have an idea of what these terms mean, and you may even be right. But what you think they mean may not be what I think they mean. Nor can you safely quote *Webster's Dictionary* definition to me as if Moses received that tome on Mount Sinai. I want to know what you think the word means so that I can understand your use of it. Such words are notoriously slippery little eels. Were the gay nineties gay? Far too many students have become adept at throwing around vague and undefined words in such a way that they can write entire papers and never have to know what their words mean. Clinton escaped impeachment by defining "sex" and "is" in ways that suited his side of the fray. He took control of the definitions. He knew.

Suppose you have been reading a book on psychology or sociology that makes heavy use of the term "repression." On the final exam, your professor asks you something about the word. Or in your final paper, you are required to discuss repression. Your first job is to define the term. You cannot safely open up your *Webster's* and quote from it. That would be much too easy. The definition may be "right" in some sense, but it may not be what is needed in order to understand the class or the text. You need to dig into your text or your class notes and find where it is defined there. You also need to find where it is used and to make sure that the author actually uses it in the way that he or she defined it. Discovering such contradictions may be the hidden puzzle of the assignment. Take nothing for granted.

I have used this assignment, and I find that it brings out both the best and the worst in students. After letting the dictionary do their work for them, students outclever themselves in another way by letting the author define the word for them. That is, they locate in the text where the word is defined and say something like, "According to author Norman Brown, 'Seperation on the outside is repression on the inside.'" Aside from the misspelling of "separation," such answers leave it up to me, the reader, to figure out what Brown meant. The sentence provides no clue whatsoever that the student has any idea. Indeed, the suspicion here is that the student is hiding behind the quotation hoping not to have to venture forth and define the term. Perhaps oral exams are a good idea after all.

Another popular evasion is to use the term but make no attempt to define it. This works well in speech when, by using a word like "deconstruct" as if we knew what we meant, we force those listening to bear the burden of having to supply the definition. By speaking confidently, we hope to avoid being put on the spot. A gullible professor might overlook this failure to define key terms. But I am not one of those saps, and you cannot count on any of us falling for this trick. Even the sweetest of us have our limits and our down days. In some cases, the initial act of defining the term can be the topic of the entire paper. Let's face it: If you can define abortion as the killing of a human infant, you barely need to go on with any more of the argument. If, on the other hand, you glibly assume that abortion is defined as the taking of a human life, and you push forward without having defended that assumption, the rest of your argument will not be worth much.

What works best is clear English speech that is free of complex subtleties or excessive jargon and that sounds like a person talking. Here is one successful definition:

Norman Brown defines repression as the action of the rational mind holding down by force, or excluding from consciousness, all of the chaotic emotions of the subconscious. Repression occurs because the human brain puts a lid on the emotions. It traps them.

Notice how this student moves from a fairly complex statement using undefined psychological terms like "consciousness" to her own simpler language, "It traps them." She presents a clear picture that is communicated from her mind to the reader's mind.

Keep Your Argument Grounded

Assuming your topic paragraph stated the argument you intend to prove, you then in the second and subsequent paragraphs need to lay out the evidence in some logical order. You want your reader to be able to follow you. So begin at a basic level at which there can be little disagreement, and take your reader by the hand up the narrow trail to the heights. Do not try to write the entire paper from the heights, but don't stay stuck on the ground either. In other words, begin with the literal and work your way to the profound, returning at the end to the rock from which you started.

This is an important tactic to master. Some students, whether answering in class, scribbling exam essays, or writing term papers, jump instantly to the lofty mountaintops of cosmic generality, leaving us earthbound clods breathless and a bit confused. Other students are mere earthworms and never lift their heads out of the soil at all. You need both: the solid earth on which we stand and the enlightened vision that we imagine separates us from the apes and ennobles us. Therefore, begin with literal facts. Begin with some solid rock from the text, some person or quotation, or perhaps with some personal experience or reaction of your own. Then slowly ascend through the circles of interpretation making sure that your reader is with you each step of the way. If you are reading *One Flew Over the Cuckoo's Nest* and you want to denounce Ken Kesey's sexism, begin by describing the examples. Then describe your reaction. Then begin to analyze

the causes both of his unbearable sexism and of your angry reaction. If you are assigned a cultural study of Easter rituals, begin
with your own family's experience. But then ascend from your
egg hunting to larger questions: Why eggs? Why do we hide
them? What do eggs and chocolate bunnies have to do with the
resurrection of Christ? Does anyone really know? If not, if we
perform rituals we cannot explain, what does that say about us?
Begin with the specific event, ask "why" often enough, and your
paper will soon be soaring through the heavens. In your conclusion, remember to refer back to the family Easter egg hunt with
which you began. Tie it all up at the end.

Refute! Reply! Fight Back!

Once you have presented your evidence and explained carefully
how that evidence proves the point you are trying to make, you
then need to take some time to refute objections. After you have
shot off your biggest guns, the enemy will still counterattack.
You must be prepared to counter those counterattacks. Include
within your paper the objections that have been or might be
raised to your argument. Try to imagine the questions that will
arise in the mind of the reader. Let the opposition tell its own
misguided story in its own voice. Show that you understand
those questions, that you have carefully considered them, and
that you have the facts and the arguments to refute them.

A paper defending abortion will have no success as an argument if it fails to acknowledge the position of those on the other
side of the debate who believe that a fetus is a human being and
that abortion therefore is murder. Say whatever you want about
a woman's right to control her own body, but as long as the
reader believes that abortion is murder, your argument will fall
on deaf ears and your paper will fail. Likewise, a paper attacking
abortion as murder needs to do more than repeat that claim.
The author must try to understand the reasoning of the other
side and then show where and why it is wrong.

If you cannot think of any opposing position, then you are in
trouble, for what you have is not an argument. If you do have an
argument but are ignorant of the opposition's views, your de-

fense will be weak. If you know the opposition's views but do not clearly understand them, then you need to do more research and apply more thought.

Conceding some territory to your opponents is always a good idea. No position is 100 percent right or 100 percent wrong; we are all sinners fumbling in the dark. Conceding that your opponent may have a point here or there will not weaken your defenses. If nothing else, this tactic tends to disarm the other side. Absolute positions that refuse to yield an inch create absolute oppositions that are equally stubborn. Surprise your readers. Be reasonable, be understanding, be sympathetic to their concerns, and then when their defenses are down, zap them with logic and club them to death with facts!

8

How to Lose Your Case

Unfortunately for you, it is easier to be critical than to be constructive. It is easier to point out mistakes than to explain how to get it right in the first place. Perhaps this is because human history is a rubble pile of mistakes waiting to be repeated, and the right answers are still a promised land somewhere over the rainbow. Whatever the reason, mistakes are easily identified and labeled. You therefore need to be able to recognize some of the most familiar logical fallacies so that you can get to them and correct them before I do.

Circular Reasoning

Circular reasoning is so prevalent that it even has its own marginal notation (mine is an arrow shaped like a circle). Indeed, its popularity is such that I feel impelled to say something about it: Don't do it!

In case you don't recognize this problem, it is the tendency to explain something by the thing explained. I have had students write on papers that "People like beef because it tastes good." This is circular. Saying they like it and saying that it tastes good are simply two ways of saying the same thing. Thus, the steak's tasting good is not the cause of liking it. In my Early American Lit class, every year someone writes that Emerson was a romantic because he lived in a romantic era. Yes, and it was a "romantic era" because romantics like Emerson lived in it. Which came first, the era or the writers in it? This too is circular reasoning.

In almost any discipline, teachers want you to see beyond the immediate facts to the cause of the phenomena, be they economic, historical, or literary problems. We live in a cause-and-effect universe. Accept the terrible truth that things do not cause themselves. In our determined world, events have causes. We expect you to search outside of the events for whatever you think might have caused them. I once heard a scholar say, "Our condition is due to the condition our condition is in." She thought she was being clever. My primary response was to wonder why she was being so evasive.

Just Say No to "Just"

To emphasize this point, I forbid the use of the j-word, "just," in any of my classes. Nothing "just" happens. Everything has a cause. Saying that something "just" happens is saying in effect that it happens without a cause. This is the kind of sloppiness we indulge in when we don't think. However difficult and at times painful, we must fight our way through the tangle to the causes. We must rattle the bars of the prison of our contingency. That is what education is for.

As a generally instructive way of illustrating this problem, I ask my students to tell me their favorite flavor of ice cream. Some say chocolate, some strawberry, some coffee, some octopus kumquat. Some claim not to like ice cream at all. Others get evasive and deny having any favorites, preferring, they say, to exercise their free will when they get into the store. Hah!

Then, having pried some sort of answer out of each student, I go back around the room asking "why." In the first round, a depressingly large number of students say, "I just do," or "It tastes good." Unwilling to let sleeping evasions lie, I keep pushing. Why does it taste good? Why does Jill over here like chocolate and Hans over there like strawberry? What are the factors that produce these differences?

A few logical positivists always fight valiantly for the illusion of free will. "Nothing forces me to choose," they say. "I make up my own mind. I am not influenced by outside factors. I am free to do what I want." But why, I respond, do you want what you want? What produces that wanting? Imagine yourself standing in front of the Baskin-Robbins counter tasting each flavor in your mind. One of them rings a louder bell in memory than others. Or perhaps you want to taste something new and different. Why do some people want to explore and experiment while others stick to the same-old same-old every time? We are all free to choose what we want, but the devil is in the wanting that precedes the choosing.

This is why little kids dragged into an ice-cream store for the first time stand at the counter in utter confusion and are unable to make up their minds. Their well-meaning parents try to be patient, but they cannot understand why Johnny can't make a choice. After all, thirty-one wonderful flavors beckon. But Johnny has no idea what any of them taste like. He has no memory to call upon. Once he has had some experience, then he will settle on a favorite.

The causes of this choice, or any choice for that matter, carry us deep into the swamp of human consciousness. All of the mysteries of human behavior suddenly come into play. Are our likes and dislikes determined by chemistry? Perhaps the caffeine in chocolate or coffee stimulates receptors in the brain. Or perhaps we are shaped by childhood experience. Maybe our first taste of strawberry ice cream occurred on a warm day in April when the world was, as the poet said, "puddle wonderful." So the cozy memories of childhood grace became associated with the flavor of strawberry until the taste experience on the tongue conjured up some faint memory of that moment with every bite. The Marxists, no doubt, can tie ice-cream preference to economic and power relationships, and the race and gender folks are working on tying their concerns to the problem.

Nothing "just" happens. Push your regression back to Adam and Eve and you still have to explain how they got there. Even the Big Bang had to be preceded by something. Some people fill the preceding void with the word "God." Others just scratch their heads. Sorry about that.

Post Hoc, Ergo Propter Hoc

This phrase is Latin for "After this, therefore because of this." We see this logical fallacy used in politics in every administration. The folks in power take credit for everything good that happens; the opposition blames them for everything bad. The 1991 recession was George Bush's doing. The booming economy of the late 1990s was Clinton's. Because some events come on the heels of or occur at the same time as some other event, we are tempted to assume cause and effect. We call the results of this behavior superstition. Depending upon superstitious circumstance to bolster your argument could be a fatal mistake.

Ad Hominem

Ad hominem attacks are attacks against people as a means of discrediting their ideas. Basically, it is a weaselly, dirty, sneaky attack. The notion that only pure, honest, sincere people can be right is a fallacy. The idea that dishonest, dirty crooks must always be wrong is another one. The attempt to discredit the Clinton health care proposal by publishing evidence of the shady financial dealings called "Whitewater" was a classic example of an ad hominem attack. If the persona can be discredited, her ideas go down in flames with her. This works in politics because people, bless them, are stupid. It does not work on term papers. Marx may have been a Eurocentric, sexist, racist, ageist pig, but his ideas stand or fall on their own merit. Melville may have beaten his wife, but what does that have to do with the mysteries of *Moby Dick*? Jefferson may have kept slaves and not really believed that "all men are created equal," but his writings on democracy are still worth studying.

Not one of us is a saint. If our ideas can be discredited by a listing of our sins, then no ideas anywhere, anytime, have any merit, not even yours. Therefore, the personal attacks come out as a wash after all the mud has been thrown. At that point, we then have to backtrack and do the hard work of considering ideas on their merits and arguments on their logic and evidence anyway. So we might as well skip the ad hominem attacks and get to work.

False Choices

Another sneaky way to try to win an argument is by putting the debate in terms of two radical extremes and forcing a false choice: "Either all Americans must some day see the light and accept Christ as their savior, or we shall all be forced to yield up our liberties to the brutal tyranny of godless communism!" Well, maybe there is a third or a fourth or several choices in between those two extremes. Presenting a stark choice between two alternatives makes a neat choice, but most of us realize that other alternatives exist.

Non Sequitur

This phrase is Latin for "It does not follow." Basically, this fallacy, like the ad hominem argument, involves the attempt to link two things together that really have little to do with each other. The problem here is that of establishing cause and effect and not settling for mere proximity. Farmers finding their cows dry once blamed the losses on the snakes they found in their barns. Their reasoning was understandable, but the conclusion was a non sequitur. An attempt to tie the financial crisis of 1836 to the rise of transcendental romanticism requires more than the mere statement of their mutual occurrence. Roosters may see a connection between their crowing and the fact of the sun's coming up. But most of us college professors are smarter than your average chicken.

Many appeals to emotion can be lumped under this category. Descriptions of atrocities by the Serbs may arouse feelings of outrage and a desire to help the Kosovo Muslims, but in any war atrocities can be found on both sides. Before we assume one side is right and worth defending, we might want to avoid jumping to hasty conclusions. It does not follow that horrific examples of atrocities by the Serbs require our intervention against them. Other factors and possibilities need to be examined.

Teleological False Assumptions

This is an all too prevalent problem.

Back in the nineteenth century, after Darwin published his *Origin of Species*, faithful Christians rejected the theory of evolution out of hand. They wouldn't even read the book. They believed in the Bible, and they believed the Bible taught that God created man directly without the use of monkeys along the way. Their minds were set on a fundamental religious conclusion that no facts, no science, no logic, no evidence, could ever sway them from. They put the conclusion they wanted to believe in first. Putting the conclusion ahead of the facts is what we call teleological thinking, from "teleology," the study of the end times.

For generations, educated people have rejected teleological thinking as somewhat backward and anti-intellectual, but it still exists today, both on the Kansas School board in its old creationist form as well as in the greatest universities in the nation in the humanities departments. There, many dogmatically committed liberals have pledged allegiance to the idea that all people are in fact created equal and that only a racist would claim to find any difference between the races, or a sexist any difference between the sexes. When a geneticist and a psychologist, using scientific studies, argued in *The Bell Curve* that there may in fact be some subtle genetic differences between blacks and whites, their book was denounced by many who refused to read it. Some, to their everlasting credit, read the book, took its claims seriously, and did the hard work of refuting it. But the well-intentioned souls who refused to read it, who knew in advance it had to be wrong, were guilty of teleological thinking as surely as were the fundamentalists at the Scopes trial. When Camille Paglia's provocative book on art and gender came out, I asked a tenured professor if she had the library's copy. She angrily responded that she would never read "that book."

To be sure, keeping an open mind can be dangerous. The world may not in the end fulfill our hopes and expectations for it. The real truth may be greater than the ideal affectation of love. But if so, then we have to know it in order to do whatever we must to change the given and construct the world we want, not insist blindly that the world is as we want it to be. Perhaps extra efforts might have to be made for some people. Perhaps women do not perform as soldiers as well as their brothers do. Maybe beef cattle do have souls. Keeping an open mind means being willing to entertain possibilities we do not like. Most teachers respect students who show an ability to be open-minded. One-dimensional propaganda papers, which push one idea from one direction only, get less regard.

Blaming the Victim

This one is a hot political potato. In some ways, it nicely illustrates the complexity of trying to untangle cause and effect and to establish responsibility in our increasingly relativistic environment.

The date-rape issue provides a good example of the problem. Is a woman who goes to a party with a fraternity brother, gets drunk, and then willingly goes up to his room responsible for what follows? To concentrate on the mistakes of the victim rather than on the crime of the perpetrator is known as "blaming the victim."

Of course, anyone with any brains ought to know better than to go to fraternity parties in the first place, but that does not justify the crime. To concentrate on the mistakes of the bimbo allows the true criminal to get away with rape. Yet where does responsibility lie? Can't the frat boy say with some justification that the girl led him on, that she responded positively every step of the way except for the final one? Indeed, a clever lawyer might well point out that the frat boy is also a victim. Since when is it okay to make derogatory assumptions about males who happen to belong to fraternities?

This argument often goes back to the social constructions of gender roles in America. Women are expected to behave in certain ways in childhood and thus are conditioned to react as they do. Are females really unable to do math, or has society conditioned them to think they are bad at numbers? If a girl flunks a calculus class, is that her fault or society's? To say it is her fault may be blaming the victim.

In that case, then, aren't men also conditioned by their sexist environment to respond as they do? If the girl is not at fault because of her conditioning, then the guy also has to be considered a victim of his conditioning. Where does that leave us? Everyone is a victim, and no one is responsible. Many people talk as if they believed that all we have to do is show how a certain antiso-

cial behavior is the result of conditioning and somehow that behavior is excused. But all behavior is the result of conditioning.
Thus, the battlefield is littered with effects, but there are no
causes between here and the horizon. Humanity continues to
wallow in its sins, but no one at all can be blamed. It's all Adam
and Eve's fault, or Eve's, or the snake's. But who put the snake up
to it?

The solution is to look at both sides, to realize that both cause
and effect exist and to take both into account. A ghetto teenager
who mugs a little old lady for her Social Security check is both a
victim of society and a perpetrator of a crime. To look only at
the cause of the behavior in social conditioning, as liberals tend
to do, or to look only at the effects of those causes in the current
moral character of the mugger, as conservatives tend to do, is to
miss the larger complexity of cause and effect working together
to produce behavior to which we attach either praise or blame. If
you can sort this mess out, you should certainly have no problem
acing your term paper.

Emotionally Logical

Appeals to emotion are almost always to be scorned, but the use
of emotion to make appeals is to be admired. To stir up emotions merely to stir up emotions is the tactic of the demagogue
who then uses those emotions for his unstated purposes. Because
of this, many teachers stress the need to be the perfect Mr.
Spock, logical to the core, all light but no heat. But this confuses
means and ends. Emotion as an end is fire raging out of control,
but your argument needs to have some fire at its core in order to
generate the energy to make the engine run.

Any argument worth making must have some emotion behind
it. At the core, we are motivated by our irrational likes and dislikes, all of which were caused by the accidental contingencies of
our births and upbringings. Our likes and dislikes, our loyalties
and enmities, our loves and hatreds, together, make us who we
are. Without them, we have no personality, no individuality. You
need to believe, or at least pretend to believe, your argument if

you are going to convince your reader. Like an actor on a stage, you have to put some heart into your act.

Do not, therefore, be afraid to burn with enthusiasm. However, be sure you have a strong argument constructed to contain the fire.

9

For Instance:
Two Examples

1—"Robert Frost:
Gentle New England Satanist"

To give you an idea of how this game can be played, let us dance through an example, not of the finished product but of the process of developing a paper topic.

Let's say you have been given the assignment to write about a poem. Let's make it one that every American schoolkid is familiar with, Robert Frost's "Stopping by Woods on a Snowy Evening." And let's assume you have no idea yet what you intend to say. Begin your writing with a simple description of the generally obvious literal facts. Make it clear that you understand the literal meaning, that indeed you read the words. We professors, cynical bastards that we are, look for that. Tell me that "Stopping by Woods" is the picture of a person riding through woods in the wintertime and stopping to "watch the woods fill up with snow." Use brief phrases or significant individual words from the text as evidence. At the very least, this proves you read the poem. Imagine a working title, something hopelessly vague like "The Meaning of Frost's Famous Poem." This at least gives you something to begin with.

Once the literal facts have been described—a fairly easy task in this example—then begin your ascent. Step beyond the literal and ask, What else might be going on here? What is suggested? What can we learn that isn't obvious?

A popular English-major approach is to describe the poet's use of one or some of the standard poetic conventions, dissonance, assonance, meter, rhyme scheme, and so on. By itself such explication is merely clever. It reveals the writer's ability to identify these conventions and to handle the jargon. But it says nothing important about the work as literature. If you wish to follow this path, you must not only reveal your ability to identify the types, but you also must say how the use of the particular convention influences the meaning of the work, how the technical structure of the poem reflects or undercuts the meaning, literal and suggested, of the words. This is difficult and subtle; the undergraduate is probably safer in sticking with the meaning of the words and not digging too deeply into the subtleties of meter and rhyme. That this poem can be sung to the tune of "Hernando's Hideaway" is an embarrassment better left to talk-show hosts or Ph.D.'s in cultural studies and prosody.

Perhaps a word or phrase of the poem suggests something not clearly spelled out in the literal facts. A popular interpretation imagines that the "who" of "Whose woods these are" is God, that "his house" in the village is the local church. If you apply this reading to the rest of the poem, it might lead to a moralistic interpretation of "miles to go before I sleep." Life, it seems, is a moral duty; if we faithfully do our moral duty, then we will be rewarded after the end. Is the poet perhaps on a pilgrimage of some sort? If so, then the literal pilgrimage of the poet's journey may stand for some other, more abstract, pilgrimage. Is life itself perhaps this pilgrimage? We must all trudge along and do our duty and not get distracted by an urge to go play in the snow. As a theme, this is pretty dull but at least possible.

But then still more ascent is possible. What is a pilgrimage? Define the term. What do we know about Robert Frost that would illuminate this idea? How does this apply to our own lives? Is Frost suggesting to us that we all go on pilgrimages? Suddenly, we find ourselves echoing Chaucer's *Canterbury Tales* and the roots of English literature. Is there a connection? Perhaps we can begin to see a pattern emerging. What does that tell us about ourselves? Perhaps the most significant thing to be learned from this poem is the way in which by responding sympathetically to this poem we (or some of us) are still caught up in the Christian worldview of our ancestors, that some (too many?) of us are still, to use the Chaucerian metaphor, Englishmen who long "to go on Pilgrimages." Isn't most of American literature—from the Pilgrims heading for their "promised land" to runaway slaves following the Big Dipper north to Jack Kerouac searching for "kicks"—a journey to we-know-not-what? As Kerouac wrote in *On the Road*, "Whither goest thou, America? Whither goest thou in thy shiny black car in the night?" What is this journey we all are on? Or if we are bored to tears by such Christian moralism, that tells us something too.

Can you then return to the poem and, rereading it with this possibility in mind, find any more hints, however subtle? Perhaps. The main action of the poem is the poet's stopping. There is at least a tension between his stopping to look at the deep dark woods and the "miles to go." The horse is said to think the stopping is not just "queer" but "a mistake." The horse of course is an animal, a possible symbol of the natural. If nature and God urge us onward to our moral duty, what then is the force that calls us to stop and contemplate the "dark and deep" woods? Some think that the temptation Frost sees is a temptation to stop all the struggles and to surrender to death on that "darkest evening of the year," a time when many people do commit suicide. If so, if life's journey is a godly responsibility, then the tempter is Satan.

That's it! Robert Frost was a Satanist! At least, he was tempted by Satanism, whatever the hell that is. The evidence is there in the poem. You can bow to the demand for strict textual interpretation and the search for a unifying theme by showing how the entire poem sets up a conflict between the call to do our godly duty and some deeper, darker impulse from the satanic forests, which themselves may be, as the wilderness often is, a symbol for the wilderness of the soul. Frost may be telling us that he is tempted by unnatural impulses from the dark side.

Or perhaps you can turn this idea on its head. If the woods are "lovely, dark and deep," perhaps they represent the divine, and Frost, with his relentless insistence on sticking to his original journey, is ignoring God's call to surrender to the mystic and is instead keeping some worldly selfish promise. In many ways, and in numerous poems, Frost illustrates the stubbornness of the modernist who believes he can put himself in control. His poem "Home Burial" is entirely the portrait of a man who is asserting his willpower over the emotions that cause his wife to lose herself entirely after the death of their child. When she threatens to run away, Frost ends the poem with his farmer shouting, "If you go, I will bring you back. I *will* . . . ." The emphasis on "will" is Frost's.

One sees the same emphasis on the will in Ahab whose soul, "by its own sheer inveteracy of will, forced itself against Gods and devils into a kind of self-assumed, independent being of its own." Hitler's great propaganda movie was called *Triumph of the Will,* and Gordon Liddy's autobiography was titled *Will.* The evil caused by the human will putting itself in control at the expense of the heart is Darth Vader's dark side of The Force. Perhaps Frost's refusal of the divine command to let go is his single-minded dedication to his own demonic will. Either way, the argument can be made and backed up with evidence and quotations. Frost was a remarkably stubborn and driven individual.

To appease the grading gods who expect you to put the poem into context, you need only skim even a brief biography of Frost. There you might learn that he once tried to kill himself in the Great Dismal Swamp, that he was considered by many to be an egomaniac and a tyrant, that he bullied his wife and children, that he pulled a gun once on his wife in front of his daughter, and that his son committed suicide. There is plenty of evidence in Frost's life, to say nothing of his many other poems, to support any argument you might like to construct about the specific evils by which he was tempted and to which he succumbed. Rumor has it that he was even a Republican.

Now that you have your interpretation, you can go back and change your working title to a more appropriate one, something like "Robert Frost: Gentle New England Satanist." Now there's an ironic title an English professor cannot resist. Then you can write your new topic sentence boldly stating the basic theme:

Although considered by many to have been a gentle New England poet of nature, Robert Frost was in fact a secret Satanist, and a close reading of such poems as "Stopping by Woods on a Snowy Evening" reveals not the godly purposefulness seen by some critics but a terrible enslavement to the Devil.

In the second paragraph, you can make use of your original effort to present your literal understanding of the surface of the poem. You need to prove to the teacher that you read and understood at least the most obvious level of the poem. Pretend you're writing for that absentminded physics professor who has been out of touch in the lab for years. Gently remind her of the basic facts, images, and words. Otherwise, your teacher will never buy your interpretation.

Be sure, always, to present objections, if only to demolish them. Imagine the voice of some sentimental sap who still clings to the pious reading of the poem. Show that you understand the objections of the disbelievers, and then show how shallow or misguided they are. Perhaps you should follow up in several more paragraphs by showing that you also have read and understand one or two of these more traditional, naive interpretations of the poem. You might want to spend a paragraph or two exploring some of the reasons those older critics missed the boat. What blinded them to the obvious? Were they part of a conspiracy to bedevil the nation's youth by foisting satanic poetry on them while pretending it had pious purposes? Or was there some way in which their self-interest was furthered by their interpretation? What was there in the old pious readings that was of benefit to these saps?

Feminists argue that the emphasis in literature classes on white male authors like Frost is part of a subtle effort to perpetuate the lie that only white male Protestants from New England have ever had anything worthwhile to say. By doing this, perhaps without realizing it, these white male professors trained in the New England tradition are reinforcing their positions of power and authority within the culture. Perhaps the moral duty Frost was recommending we all stick to, presumably, was the oppressive demand that blacks stay in the fields and women stay in the kitchen, As a white male New England Protestant myself, I find this line of reasoning utterly ridiculous, but I have to grant that it is a perfectly possible argument to try to make.

Among other perfectly possible, if utterly ridiculous, interpretations, Marxists might talk about Frost's marketing and "commodifying," as they say, his art, which certainly goes along with his Republican politics. The emphasis on ownership, "his house . . . his woods . . . my little horse . . . But I have . . . ," suggests an obsession with control and possession. Frost, so his biographers tell us, was a careful man with a penny who kept every scrap of paper he doodled on to sell to equally materialistic collectors. Feminists can explore his role as patriarchal tyrant and defender of traditional male hegemonic values. What, after all, do we make of the unrelenting repetition of "his house," "his woods," "his harness bells"? African Americans might want to explore Frost's use of "darkness" as a signifier for evil. The gay practitioners of "Queer Studies," as they, in their Yankee Doodle way, now call it, can do a real number on Frost based on his horse's opinion. Clearly, the interpretive possibilities are almost limitless. There is even a school of interpretation, certainly beneath my contempt, whose adherents argue that what is left out is really what a work is all about, that our silent denials reveal our true selves. If no mention is made of global warming or of apartheid in South Africa, that could be significant. Just what is Frost trying to hide, anyway, and why is he trying to hide it?

That nonsense aside, one of the main attractions of the poem, as is true of all great literature from the Bible through *Moby Dick* to *Thelma and Louise*, is that it is specific enough to be interpreted but vague enough to allow you to project your own concerns onto it. You need to remember not to succumb to either extreme but to retain both text and context. You do not want to surrender your own insights in favor of some deep inner meaning cleverly hidden in the text, but neither do you want to leave the text behind as you chase after your personal or ideological butterflies.

Once the naive, sentimental reading of the poem has been dealt with, or the cynical, oppressive implications of the poem have been exposed, you can go on and reveal by a close reading just how you arrived at your terrifying revelation. Here, you need to bring in whatever other clues you can find in your reading of the rest of the poem. To whom did Frost make those "promises to keep"? And what might those promises have been? Perhaps Frost sold more than scraps of paper. How great a price might an ambitious man pay for fame and literary power? What now happens to the repetition of the last line, "and miles to go before I sleep"? Instead of a holy pilgrimage, is this perhaps a satanic mission? And doesn't the lockstep repetition of that last line send a chill through the reader's soul?

In later paragraphs, you can bring in the outside facts from Frost's life, or perhaps some evidence from one or two of his other poems (what was that "other road" in the yellow wood less traveled by?). For these, you may have to quote biographers, literary critics, class notes. You may have to use your imagination. But as long as your reasoning is logical and the evidence valid, who can call you wrong?

Near the end, you need to say something about the "use" of your revelation, that is, the significance for us all. You might add an appropriately chilling message. Perhaps we should be less naive. Satan is everywhere. Let us reexamine Daffy Duck and Mickey Mouse: Capitalists? Yes. Sexists? Certainly. But Satanists? That had gotten by us before. Quick, run to the den and turn off the TV before another generation of Americans is corrupted.

Remember these rules: Present your arguments, define your terms, present your evidence, explain how your evidence proves your argument, and don't forget to include opposing views that you then demolish. To present only one side of an issue is unconvincing and ultimately becomes propaganda rather than a balanced argument. You need to take the counterarguments into account. This has the additional advantage of making it appear as if you have greater control over the whole of the debate. Even if you are wrong it gives your paper more authority. If you have time and ambition and want to go beyond the usual sophomore paper, quote from some published analysis of the poem to prove you are not attacking some straw man.

At the end of the paper, conclude with a paragraph that sums up your basic argument. Do not try to bring new evidence or new ideas into the conclusion. If you have more to say, or a new idea, go back and put it into the body of the paper where it belongs. And in your concluding paragraph, refer back to the topic paragraph, to the beginning of the paper with some allusion to the language or the imagery of the opening. This brings your paper full circle and neatly ties it up in a tightly closed bundle. Restate your argument and your conclusion. Drive the stake finally deep into Frost's cold heart, and nail down the coffin lid. Read the poem again; then lock the door.

2—"Women Are Like Boxcars"

The paper reproduced in this section is a real one. That is to say, it was written not by me—I swear!—but by a student in one of my college composition classes. Mr. Beard, the student author, is a representative of that pervasive southern species, cousins of which can be found throughout the fifty states, called *Redneckus Americanus*. Only kudzu, honeysuckle, and poison ivy are more resistant to cultivation or eradication. Over six feet and built like a refrigerator, he was the type of guy who causes the tractor to tilt when he climbs on it. His papers tended to smell of the stuff he had clinging to his boots when he stomped into class. But they also had a distinctive voice, an enviable clarity, straightforward logic, good organization, and fair to virtuous grammar. What is more, given the political atmosphere in academia today, he took dangerous risks. Horrified though I sometimes was at the content of his essays, I had to love them.

This particular assignment came at the end of a few weeks during which the class had been reading several different versions of the Cinderella story along with a number of essays analyzing the stories from different perspectives. The feminist take on Cinderella, a dominant theme of the exercise, was underscored by our viewing of a recent feminist film version in which Cinderella is a rugged tomboy and the prince a complete fop who needs Cindy's superior strength and fighting abilities to save him. All I asked the students to do was to produce for me a three- to five-page paper giving me their take on the whole thing. As usual, I told them, I would be looking for a clear argument, backed up by logic and evidence from the text. And that was all I said. I wanted to leave it up to them to have their say.

Mr. Beard's paper was among the very best, not just because of its vigorous and dangerous argument, but because he went beyond the texts read in the class, beyond literary or even feminist journals, to bring in evidence from the social sciences, research that went beyond what was expected. Had this been a paper for a social science class, the tone would not have endeared him to the professor. Nor would the number of studies cited have been enough to validate his argument. But his use of scientific studies of this sort, even in a paper for an English class, demonstrates the cross-disciplinary liberties that English professors, at least, like to see.

Here, then, with my original handwritten marginal comments, is the paper. Plagiarize it, or even imitate it, at your own risk. As for Mr. Beard, perhaps emboldened by his success in my English class, perhaps tired of life on the farm, he left his shit-kickers at home after graduation and was accepted, with a scholarship, into law school. If he can write a paper like this and not merely survive but thrive, so can you.

The title, correctly spaced a third of the way down a title page, was "Woman Are Like Boxcars: A Study of the Cinderella Myth."

1

run-on

"Women are like boxcars they all are just writing around waiting to get

shows

hitched." This line from the Sanford and Sons television show ~~and~~ I believe that

Red Fox has found a psychological truth. The reason why the story of Cinderella

has become so popular and prolific is ~~(the across the board recognition of)~~ the fact

It is the Fact, not the recognition Sin Boldly!

that all women are awaiting their savior, who is a man, to deliver them from their

boring little lives. Their knight in shining armor is the only one who can save

them from their timid little feminine prisons. They not only need him, but they

really want him.

Not everyone will agree with my argument that all women need and want a

man to raise them up and out of their terrible little existences. It's Marion Young,

guess

who you can tell by the way she kept her maiden name, is one of those short-

haired women. She has published many articles in journals such as the Socialist

underline or italicize Pub'd titles

Review and Valley Woman's Voice. She boasts articles with such names as

Cite Source

"Socialist Feminism and the Limits of Dual System Theory" and other such

s

motorcyle-riding, butch nonesense. She would argue that "some would say that

the real differences in behavior and psychology between men and women can be

attributed to some natural and eternal feminine essence but every human

existence is defined by its situation; the particular existence of the female person

is no less defined by the historical, cultural, and economic limits of her situation"

a

(Young 142). Oh, yes! You go, girl! A woman can do anything!

I agree with Ms. or Mrs. or Mr. Or whatever Young that women can do

and succeed in anything but I also contend that deep down inside of them they

but is this from nature or nurture? How'd it get there?

2

want a big strong man to sweep them off of their feet, a great man to take care *NAS*
of them and guide them through the rest of their lives, a John Wayne to build *NAS*
them a house "at the bend in the river where the cotton woods grow," a Red *NAS*
Butler to "frankly my dear I don't give a damn," a Humphrey Bogart to "here's *NAS*
looking at you, kid." These stories do not just come out of an era they are instead *run-on*
a masculine and feminine inherent quality that is more instinctive than cinematic.

Steven Goldberg an incredible doctor of psychology, has proven that *?*
"everyone – even most people describing themselves as feminists – understands
that physiological differentiation plays some part in differentiating male and
female behavior" (Goldberg 3). He *argues* shows that the reason why feminists are
feminists is because they clearly "value masculine qualities more highly than
feminine ones" (Goldberg 12). He goes on to show how the reliance women have
on men is paramount to the survival of the human race. Women have a primary
important purpose and that is to have and raise their children. If this is, as
Goldberg affirms, their single most important function then they must rely on
men for fertilization and protection while dedicating their entire time to
performing this function. The men also bring home the groceries to nourish the
entire family. These functions are part of our inherent instincts. If they were not,
then our species would never have survived. *this needs a transition*

Men naturally possess three qualities. They are "competitiveness ..., relative
suppression of other emotions and needs and a sacrifice of rewards that compete
with the need for attainment and dominance, and actions required for attainment
of position, status, and dominance" (Goldberg 65-66). If women were equal or

[handwritten margin note: introduce quotes. identify author in your text]

the same as men competition would have destroyed our race. Men naturally

dominate. They were created to. "In a world dominated by men, the world of

men is, by definition, a world of power. That power is a structured part of the

[handwritten margin note: block that quote!]

economies and systems of political and social organization; it forms part of the

core of religion, family, forms of play, and intellectual life. On a individual level,

much of what we associate with masculinity hinges on a man's capacity to

exercise power and control (Kaufman 142).

Women are waiting for a powerful and dominant man to come and save

them but it has to be a big and strong man. The reason for this is the same reason

[handwritten margin note: Says who?]

badgers have. A female badger seeks the biggest and strongest male to mate with

so he will protect her and her young. Elephants do the same. This also ensures

the best genes are passed on throughout the race. It makes perfect sense. The

species grows in population as well as individual strength. The society is formed

and it prospers.

Trying to say that this is no longer necessary and women can now do all of

the things a man can is a poor attempt at humor. The fact is that this genetic

[handwritten margin note: monkeys]

[handwritten margin note: good! some evidence]

formula is engrained in our being. Tests conducted on adolescent males show

these inherent qualities are present even when not taught or observed in society.

[handwritten margin note: What does all this mean?]

A composite score of three reactivity measures from both novelty tests was a
poor predicator of pretransfer and one year posttransfer dominance, but a
good predicator of dominance two years posttransfer. These results
demonstrate a potential role for male rhesus macaques'; dispositional
characteristics in shaping the outcome of dominance interactions once males
emigrate from their natal groups. (Wallen)

4

Yeah, exactly Dave and Kim, Boys will be boys, won't they? Years of research have proven this old adage. It is in their genetic make-up.

This is the same as the reason why all women are searching for the perfect man to come and save them. Just as the very wise television show "Friends" showed us, "A man plans a wedding for maybe a month while a woman plans it her whole life." The reason so many women flock to stories like *Cinderella* or *Prince Charming* or *Titanic* is because they are recreations of the dream they have been having since they were born. This recreation is of their inner most dream and desire come to life. They ~~NAS~~ love and revel in its glory. They sing and dance along with Cinderella after she wins the love of the prince and they sob uncontrollably when their man freezes to death in the wreckage of such a great ship. These stories are so proliferate because they strike *was.* ? a cord of our very being and this also explains why stories like *Cinderella* are timeless and cross all cultural and language barriers. They are a constant for the whole human race. They should be understood and embraced for what they are Recreations of the A- dreams of our very essence and not just some fairy tale.

good

Not to reward sexist pigism, but how can I argue with a strong colorful voice, a clear argument, and fairly well-cited references. The counter argument could be more fully developed, especially here. You do include Ms Young, but what would she say in response to your argument? Clean the mechanics, learn to use commas, and next time you'll get an A.

Works Cited

Goldberg, Steven, *Why Men Rule: A Theory of Male Dominance* Open Court, ✓ Chicago, 1993.

Kaufman, Michael, "Men, Feminism, and Men's Contradictory Experiences of ✓ Power" in Brod, Harry, and Kaufman, Michael *Theorizing Masculinities* SAGE , 1994.

Young, Iris Marion, *Throwing Like A Girl and Other Essays in Feminist* ✓ *Philosophy and Social Theory,* Indiana University Press, Bloomington, 1990.

Where's a Citation for the Walton quote? What happened to "Dave + Kim"? Why nothing from the net? How old-Fashioned. A quote from Cinderella might've been nice too.

10
Literary Games

The "Deep Inner Meaning" Debate

Once upon a time, when the world was young, literature teachers lectured on the biographical details of the lives of the great authors and discussed in broad, general terms how their ideals furthered the values and visions of the nation. After the literary rebellions of the early 1900s, new tools became available to help us understand ourselves. When Freudian psychotherapy became a fad in the roaring 1920s, literary critics started to see phallic symbols everywhere. In the 1930s, with the onset of the Great Depression, intellectuals turned from sex to economics to find out what really pulls our strings. During that era, Marxism replaced Freudianism as the theoretical lens through which literature was read. In the 1940s and 1950s, a group of scholars, wearied to tears by all that pompous "literary history" of the previous century and the trendy fads of the previous two decades, began to insist that close readings of the text alone ought to be the subject of scholarly concern. These "New Critics," as they were called, judged the texts under their scrutiny for internal thematic organization, which they called "unity," and for internal paradoxes, subtle allusions, and verbal nuance, full of classical, mythological, and religious significance. Rejecting earlier approaches, they took up the battle cry that a text was a text and only the text itself mattered, that the reader should not care if a poem were written in China before Christ or yesterday in the Bronx.

Literary and historical studies owe these New Critics considerable credit for rescuing us from the oxygen-starved heights of
noble generalities and the doctrinaire obsessions of the Freudians and Marxists. The New Critics may have rejected the old
tradition of bringing outside interests to the text, but they more
than made up for it by finding profound depths of meaning in
the subtle internal details and symbolic suggestions. They deserve huzzahs for emphasizing close readings of the text, readings in which a student studies a paragraph or sentence and
carefully analyzes each word as if it were a multifaceted prism
reflecting a different color on each face and then comparing
words to words within the same text. But students also have the
New Critics to blame for the mind-numbing search for some secret, hidden, "deep inner meaning" that all too often seems to be
what college professors are asking for.

In the 1960s, a passion for the political concerns surrounding
texts came in with the passionate politics of the era. No longer the
tool of stuffy old literary historians or party-line Stalinists, concern
for relevance and historical context brought history and biography
back to the study of literature with a new sense of purpose. Suddenly it mattered considerably if an author were white or black,
male or female, WASP or Asian, gay or straight, rich or poor, a
hawk or a dove. The New Critics became an enemy to be denounced for failing to make the study of literature relevant to the
struggles for civil rights and against the Vietnam War. Worse,
some seemed complicit in defending traditional views about race
and society. That some of the most vocal New Critics were agrar-
ian Southerners with conservative views about race and neo-
orthodox views of religion has done little to help their reputation.

The old order had assumed that American culture could be
defined in terms of some consensus, that we were in fact a melt-
ing pot in which most of our differences had been transformed
into a new whole. In the face of the Depression and then attacks
by fascist madmen both in Europe and in the Pacific, an understandable rallying around the flag did forge an appearance of su-
perficial unity. In the 1960s, that appearance was shattered.
Suddenly, objectivity itself came into question, only to be replaced by a diversity of competing subjective viewpoints. We
still have not picked up all the pieces.

As a result of this move, students began to have a choice. No longer restricted to discovering the one great secret meaning that a close reading of the text revealed, nor any longer subservient to the intention of the author, students began to explore different approaches to talking about texts. They could take a New Critical approach and look for deeper meaning solely within any given text if they wanted to, or they could examine some of the circumstances of the writing of the text, or they could analyze their own or others' reading of the text. My disciplinary field of American Studies arose in opposition to the New Critics with a determination to restore the internal details of the text to their worldly context. Today, we have fled so far from the New Critics that the text itself is often abandoned in critical analysis or at least lost against the background of gender and racial politics. Indeed, to some of my fellow refugees from Woodstock, still "personing" the barricades of Birmingham, race and gender are all that matter, and the study of a text has become an excuse for political sermons on the sins of the world. To "contextualize" originally meant to read a text not as a thing unto itself alone but within the many circumstances of its world. It has come to mean "Look at the text from my perspective." Just as some New Critics veered too far from context into the text and lost all connection to the real world, some professors today tend to plunge too far into context and lose all connection to the text. To them, to contextualize means "Forget the text and listen to me." But the best scholars, then and now, look at both text and context and tie the internal dynamics of the text to their broader cultural and political significance.

Searching for Symbols

"When correctly viewed," sang Tom Lehrer, "everything is lewd," and anyone who has ever laughed at a dirty joke knows that language is full of double meanings with symbolic reference. Indeed, we are ourselves all symbols, and everything around us radiates with symbolic meaning. Colors, shapes, images, sounds, smells, all sensory experience, stimulate associations and memories. These thoroughly subjective impressions and fleeting associations are the meat of what we call symbols. Even if we are not

conscious of the associations in the backs of our minds that at-
tract us and repel us, those unconscious symbolic meanings are
there. As Emily Dickinson said, "'Tis not revelation that awaits
but our unfurnished eyes." Behind the literal surface, meanings
lurk everywhere if only we have the eyes to see them. Too close
attention to the immediate details can obscure the larger significance of what is going on. Both type and antitype, the immediate
literal and the broad symbolic, are always there. When John
Wayne Bobbitt's Latin American wife cut off his penis with a
carving knife, the macho image of America that John Wayne
once personified suffered its final blow. It was a powerfully symbolic moment. The great symbol maker who is always, as Kurt
Vonnegut says, busy, busy, busy had done it again.

What, after all, is a tie? Why do men wear a piece of cloth
around their necks? Is it to hide the buttons? What is the symbolic meaning of a tie? Ties are first of all masculine objects;
men wear them. They are also symbols of authority, which is a
form of power. World leaders, lawyers, businessmen, men who
expect to be taken seriously, all wear them. So ties are long narrow objects that hang down in the middle of men's bodies and
are symbols of masculine power. They tend to be pointed too.
Those squared, cutoff ties can be found in the backs of the racks,
but they are clearly less popular. Maybe John Bobbitt wears one.
And what about bow ties? Aren't they usually associated with a
Mr. Peeper's nerdy wimpiness? You get the point.

In Slovakia, where I labored for a year trying to bring American culture to the recently liberated victims of a socially constructed utopia, I was startled to learn that on the morning after
Easter, men and boys carrying homemade whips traditionally
visit the homes of women. When the females open the door, the
males whip them across the back and then throw perfumed wa-
ter on them. Then the females, to make the symbolic game complete, hand the guys Easter eggs. And as if that isn't bad enough,
the mothers then reward the guys for symbolically impregnating
their daughters by handing out candy to the kids and booze to
the older guys. When I suggested that this ritual had obvious
sexual symbolism, my Slovakian students were outraged. "You
decadent Westerners see sex everywhere," I was told. I couldn't
deny it. But when asked what the ritual meant, the students told

me they did it because their ancestors did it. And why did their ancestors do it? I innocently asked. Because their ancestors before them did it; that's why! They were not ready to admit that this ritual might have arisen with symbolic meanings long since lost in the fog of time and kept alive by the enduring power of that unconscious symbolism. They clung to the literal.

Our clothes and our rituals are thus full of symbolic meaning, and so are our words and texts. We all recognize status symbols like expensive cars. What about the many ways different groups try to make themselves look cool: the grunge look, the prep look, the cornrow hair, the dreadlocks? Whether intentional or unintentional, these are all symbols. They all have unspoken meanings. So do the clothes, the words, and the actions of persons in texts and in history. Finding symbolic meanings is simply a matter of seeing beyond the literal and being willing to let your imagination run free. Think of your text as one of those holusion posters sold in the malls in which, after you gaze cross-eyed for a few minutes, the surface pattern dissolves to reveal an open window onto a previously unseen picture. Sometimes, symbolic meanings seem to be revealed to us; more often, we bring our own interpretations to them. No one right symbolic interpretation exists. We each see through different lenses.

Sticking to the traditional meanings that have historically been associated with traditional symbols can even get you into trouble. Recently, the African American novelist Alice Walker was named a California "state treasure" and presented with a sculpture of a nude woman's torso. Those presenting the award saw this plaster Venus as a symbol of classical art. Walker, who had just written a book on female mutilation, was outraged at what she saw as "a decapitated, armless, legless woman, on which my name hung from a chain." Such figures may symbolize art to some, she said, but to her they symbolize "domination, violence, and destruction." After insulting her fans, Walker decided to keep the award, but she keeps it in a box.

Note the brouhaha over the Confederate battle flag, the Stars and Bars. Unreconstructed Southerners claim it is "just" a symbol of their heritage. The NAACP sees it as a symbol of white supremacy and segregation. A few of us Boston Yankees still see the flag as a banner of treason under which rebels once rose in arms to destroy the United States. We see in its tilted cross the lives of 360,000 patriotic boys who died to prevent a bumpkin feudalism based on slavery from destroying the last best hope for man on earth. Whose reading of this symbol is right? A New Critical approach might ignore the politics and concentrate instead on the colors and design of the flag itself. The rest of us can only marshal our best arguments to persuade our readers of our readings of these symbols. This process includes using logic and evidence to convince the reader to see our story not necessarily as the only right one but as the one most relevant to the reader's concerns. We have to make our interest his or hers using all the literary gimmicks we have.

When an author comes right out and tells you that a necklace is "like" a slave's chain or that a tie is "like" a penis, we call that a simile: A is "like" B. When the author never makes the symbolic meaning explicit but throws out clues and hints, we call that a metaphor. In Ken Kesey's *One Flew Over the Cuckoo's Nest*, Mc-Murphy gives up his life to liberate his friends. Even without the electrodes placed on his head like a crown of thorns or the table shaped like a cross or the twelve disciples who go fishing with him, we recognize McMurphy as a Christ symbol and his death as an extended metaphor for the crucifixion.

Nor are we restricted to the symbolic meanings intentionally stuck in by some author; writers themselves do not always know why they do what they do. That is why critics can get away with saying that a text is really all about something else of which the author had nary a clue. Is the hunt for the great white Whale really about addiction to cocaine? Is Madonna really a symbol of piety and not sacrilege? Who knows? Indulge your suspicions. Follow the clues and see where they lead.

This ability to read symbolically, to view the very world around us symbolically, is at the heart of the whole literary game. To accept things at first glance to be as they appear on the surface is to be trapped in the literal. To be able to see symbolic possibilities allows one to begin to make connections between things that at first seem to have little to do with each other. Freud thought everything pointed to sex, but even the silliness of sex is itself a symbolic game. *Thelma and Louise* is not just about two women. These two symbolize all women escaping a sexist world. But they also symbolize all people escaping any entrapment in the text. The world is, as the Puritan poet Edward Taylor wrote, "slic't up in types." If we are ever to escape the text, we need to follow the symbols outward.

"As Jonas was three days in the belly of the whale," says Jesus, "so shall the son of man be three days in the belly of the Earth." A fundamentalist who insists that the story of Jonah is to be read literally will have a hard time explaining this line. But someone who sees that Jonah's experience is a symbol of extreme self-denial, as is the cross, can make the connection. The children of Israel fleeing Egypt are but one more historical event if read literally. Read symbolically, the tale of their escape from Egypt becomes an escape of the soul from any tyranny, political or ideological or emotional. An addict escaping addiction or Thelma and Louise escaping their boring lives can see themselves in the Old Testament text. Symbols tend to be flexible enough to allow us to identify across space and time. But to be open to them, we need to have open minds and to use our imaginations.

That was what Charles Manson did. Whatever may be said about his or his followers' murderous deeds, Manson's interpretation of the Beatles' *White Album* in terms of the Book of Revelations and the racial politics of the 1960s was brilliant. Had he been an English professor at Berkeley, the school would have awarded him tenure, a different sort of life sentence from the one he now serves. Manson clearly understood that the imagination needs to leave the literal behind. "The original sin," he said, "was to write it down." Nor was he tied by any narrow adherence to authorial intent. When he was asked if the Beatles really intended all that he read into their lyrics, his response was as modern as the latest lit-crit theory: "I don't know whether they did or not. But it's there. It's an association in the subconscious. This music is bringing on the revolution, the unorganized overthrow of the Establishment. The Beatles know in the sense that the subconscious knows."

The other lesson of the Manson example is one you already know: Following the threads of one's imagination into the labyrinth of the mind might lead not to the promised land but into the bottomless pit. The wilderness of ideas can be both an exciting and a dangerous place. There are definitely risks there.

But if we bravely face the risks, and avoid the pit that Manson fell into, we might even be among those who cross the frontier and break on through to Canaan.

Texts in Context

Years ago there was a musical comedy about a girl in a circus who fell in love with the puppets but hated the puppeteer. She was a bit confused, and it took the whole damn play and a lot of noisy songs before she figured out that the puppets were in fact aspects of the man she thought she hated. Eventually, she learned to love the man too.

Being a child of the 1960s, I never could sympathize with that girl or her problem, and I have an equally hard time sympathizing with any New Critic who writes about a book or a poem as if the book or the poem was a world unto itself and not an extension of some author who in turn is part of some larger historical and cultural context. Even a history text exists as an act of some historian's imagination. Certainly, all texts have to be dealt with on their own terms, and we need to avoid the tyranny of accepting the author's intention as the only interpretation possible, but to ignore the puppeteer who is making the characters talk is naive. One can ask why a certain character in a book does something. But one can also push the analysis back a step and ask why the author makes that character act that way. And one can then go a step further and ask what it is that makes that author make that character act that way. The title page bearing the original publication date is one of the most important pages in any book. That Longfellow's "Midnight Ride of Paul Revere" was written in 1861 suggests that the poem may have more to do with the politics of the Civil War than the mythology of the American Revolution.

Forty years ago, the New Critics argued that context is irrelevant, that a poem should be appreciated entirely for its own sake, and that it should not matter who wrote it or when or why. Today this view seems quaint. Textual voices are extensions of human voices, which are themselves extensions of ideologies, races, genders, religions, and all the other interest groups that constitute culture. William Faulkner once said in response to a question that he had no responsibility for what the characters in his books did or said. But he was drunk at the time. In response to outraged critics of *The Awakening*, Kate Chopin said that she "never dreamed of Mrs. Pontellier making such a mess of things" and that by the time she found out "what she was up to" it was too late. I have no idea what her excuse was for such evasive nonsense.

So when you are trying to think of something to write about, be sure to lift your eyes from the page. If you can think of nothing to say about the book, think about the way in which people or problems are presented in the book. Are the ways in which different people are represented fair? Are the presentations stereotypes or are they believable? Even if unfair and unbelievable, are they nonetheless compelling? Why? Think about the context of the writing of the book. Why did Harriet Beecher Stowe make Uncle Tom so good and noble? Who was her audience? Was she effective? Is she still? Tom's nobility may have meant one thing to her white audience in the 1850s and other things to other audiences later. How has the context changed, and how does that change our appreciation of the book today? Remember also that the main character, or the most noble character, need not be an extension of the author. Indeed, the author may have put no one in the book except characters he or she hated. Do not assume that the voice of the work is the true voice of the author. Writers, as I hope you realize by now, often fake it.

Because I think in pictures, I like to imagine this problem as a series of concentric rings, as illustrated here. The circle in the middle of the bull's-eye is the text, either the book, the phrase, or the action or object or personality under study. The first circle around it is the presentation of the object, how it is depicted, both what the author may have intended at that particular time and how the presentation appeared to her readers. The two perspectives, after all, may be quite different. The next circle is the author. Who is the person who created these images and stories? Does knowing the author help us to understand why the characters or events are presented as they are? This leads to the next circle, which is the author's immediate context. Just as we ask who the author is to get an idea of why the text appears as it does, so too we can ask about the author's personal context, what

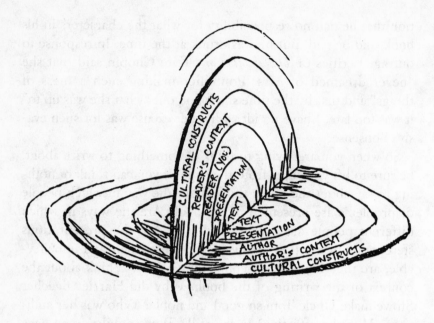

were the issues important to her at that time, to get an idea of why she writes as she does. Around that circle, then, is the larger worldview or structure within which the author's context needs to be understood, the culture, nationality, class, or whatever other historical contingency that shaped that author's life. Beyond that is the cosmic background, the larger dimensions of meaning that speak across space and time to all of us.

For instance, to understand something in *Uncle Tom's Cabin*, we might simply look at Uncle Tom and ask why he is so good; or we might expand to the first circle and ask why Harriet Beecher Stowe made Uncle Tom so Christlike; or we might continue this expansion and ask who Stowe was, what she believed, and why. This might lead us to a discussion of her role as a daughter rebelling against a patriarchal father or to analysis of the Romantic rebellion against Calvinism in Victorian American culture. In either case, we might then ask about the role of blacks as symbols in the white American mind, a discussion that in turn could open up the whole concept of symbolic consciousness. For every answer, we can find another "why" to ask that can lead to another level waiting to be explored.

Next, we need to imagine that cutting across this two-dimensional series of concentric rings is another series of rings coming up at us out of the page. This becomes our personal reading of the text, which is still in the center. Rather than exploring the context of Stowe's creation of the novel, we might find it more interesting to explore the context of our own reading of the novel. Thus, instead of asking why Stowe made Tom such a Christlike sufferer, you might ask, "Why do I react as I do, either positively or negatively, to this image?" And you can also take this to the next level and ask, "Okay, who am I? How does who I am affect my reading of the text?" Hence, a black person may well respond differently from a white person, or a male from a female, or a Baptist from an atheist. Whether a black Baptist female is more attracted by the Christian themes or more repulsed by the racial images could tell that person a lot about herself. In this new series of circles, you the reader are the author of your particular reading of the text. And it is perfectly acceptable for you to analyze your own reading of the text instead of Stowe's writing of it. Perhaps you could do a comparison and contrast of both.

Although such personal readings are in fact very much in vogue these days, some teachers object to this approach as being far too subjective. In deference to them, and to prevent your essay from losing sight of the text in some polemic about slavery or racism or the need for all sinners to be born again, it is a good idea to keep the text in view and to keep your interpretation of even your own responses orbiting around it.

Cynics and Essentialists

Knowing something about some of the current academic debates can help you approach the problem of finding a topic in ways that will impress your grader. These debates are nothing new. Solomon said that "all is vanity"; St. Paul affirmed that we "see through the glass darkly"; Calvin proclaimed that the human mind "is a perpetual factory of idols." But every generation worth its salt reinvents the wheel and calls it by a new name. Keeping up with the language of criticism, knowing which trendy words to use, is important. The successful academic lives off the fad of the land.

Any texts, whether history or literature or works of art, can be approached at face value as if they express their own meaning, or they can be approached as if they are artful manipulations that serve some ulterior end. Those who believe in the importance of the intention of the author, the meaning of the text, or the eternal beauty of a work of art are called "essentialists." Like all romantics, they believe that truth and beauty really are present in the text and in our lives. Essentialists believe there is an inherent "essential" reality deep within each person and each text, a truth waiting to be found. Rationalists, too, are basically essentialist, for they also believe a reality exists that science and logic can reveal. The difference is that rationalists believe the head can know this truth, whereas romantics believe only the heart can. But both believe that we humans can know reality.

Cynics, on the other hand, tend to believe that either rationalist or romantic readings of texts are much too innocent. The heart, they say, is a socially constructed behavioral response, and the head merely rationalizes what has been programmed into the heart. They see no transcendent absolute but only a world of shifting allegiances and interests. The Constitution, they say, was not a "miracle at Philadelphia" but the worldly compromise of a group of self-interested politicians trying to figure out a way to keep their friends and fortunes on top. Beauty, they say, is an emotional reaction in the eye of the beholder that is dependent upon the beholder's needs and wants. Love is a glandular condition. To them, the self is a socially constructed illusion, a product of the conservative forces that hold society together and shape each new person to a standard mold. These hardened spirits believe there is no spirit, no common human self, no essential truth behind the veil, only the endless materialist bumping together of random atoms. Thus, to them everything is relative: There is no such thing as Truth, but different people of different social groups, genders, religions, and classes will see different things and call them true. Females are not essentially more emotional or mothering than males, they say. This is a myth constructed by males to keep women in their place. Any endorsement of such essential qualities, they properly point out, suggests a not-so-subtle racism or sexism. Even science, some argue, is another socially constructed myth. They quote that cynical scientist Ben Franklin: "So wonderful a thing it is to be a rational creature, for a rational creature can find a reason for anything he has a mind to do."

While essentialists approach a text looking for some larger truth or beauty, cynics approach the same text asking how it was constructed, by whom, why, and for whose benefit. They reject aesthetics outright, damning any discussion of beauty as a naive evasion of the financial or political factors that make some things appear "beautiful" and not others. Their interpretations stress the literal and political realities and show the more abstract religious or philosophical approaches. They do not even believe in their own inner selves, seeing all "selves" as but socially constructed personas, and so they try to unwrap their own conditioning if only to get some sense of what makes them tick. Such people, says James Baldwin, have "no touchstone for reality. For this touchstone can be only oneself. Such a person interposes between himself and reality nothing less than a labyrinth of . . . historical and public attitudes." No wonder so many intellectuals are neurotic Woody Allens always analyzing themselves and then analyzing their analysis.

Take either approach, but be prepared to defend yourself from the other side. To come up with a topic, carefully read the text and consider the assignment. If you can't find some intrinsic meaning or beauty you want to discuss, then take a constructionist view and ask as Cicero did in the Roman Senate, *"Cui bono?"* To whom the good? Who benefits? Who loses? Why is this text constructed the way it is? Why do people respond to it as they do?

Many texts, especially in American literature, deal with this very theme of whether the self is a product of the social constructions of civilization along the shore or some essential nature to be found in the lonely depths of the soul on a raft adrift down the Mississippi. Should Edna Pontellier have stayed home and created a meaning for her life among her friends and family? Was she running away from responsibility, or was she escaping the structural cage in order to find some essential freedom when she stripped naked and swam into the depths of the sea?

Money is a good example of this theme. The dollar bills in our wallets are socially constructed fictions. They only seem to have value; they are in fact merely pieces of paper with writing on them. Their value is apparent, not real. Their value is not in the paper but in the story we believe about the paper, and even that is not something we are born with but is something we learn as we grow up. Still, even those who insist that our perceptions of reality and our sense of value are socially constructed and therefore false will not open their wallets and hand out the bills therein. It may be artificial and constructed and self-interested, but we live in this fallen realm. Ten-dollar bills may be, in some true sense, "just" paper, but I'll continue to value the few in my wallet as if they were real anyhow. The world exists even if it is an illusion.

Until the Second Coming or the destruction of the "matrix," we seem to be stuck with this illusion whether or not we believe an essential truth exists behind the mask. As Norman O. Brown so beautifully put it, "The Fall is into language." The question is whether we accept these artificial constructions, change them, or try to escape. Some clearly need to be changed; some clearly can't be. But no such change is truly liberating. Most are little more than a change of cage. To trade capitalism for Marxism would simply be to substitute a chaotic market brainwashing for a centrally controlled brainwashing. Personally, I'd rather be brainwashed by the random forces that are responsible for the evolution of the species and the nation-state and the Internet than by the elitist experts who imagine they can construct something better. Indeed, if we make the matrix too comfortable, we may lose all desire to break free, forget that we are in a cage, and, in effect, return to slavery in Egypt. Perhaps, like Huck, we need to resist the comforts of civilization and light out for the territory.

If you can understand this debate and apply it to the text, whether the author invites you to or not, whether the assignment specifically calls for it or not, you should do well on any college paper.

RaceGenderClass

The latest thing in literary criticism is a confusion called "deconstruction," itself only the most visible dogma in a larger rela-

tivism known as "postmodernism." At its simplest, it can be
thought of as a way to break down a text to reveal not its essential meaning, for deconstructionists say no such thing exists, but
how it works politically to enhance the power of some or to oppress others. Many American deconstructionists, and their many
variants, having an affinity for left-wing politics, seized on this
French import after the 1960s as a weapon with which to continue the New Left's attempts to bring the establishment to its
knees. In 1968, they tried to trash Chicago; today, grown mid-
dle-aged and tenured, they are still trying to bring the traditional white male culture to its knees. Deconstructionists and
their allies in Cultural Studies comb over texts of the Dead
White European Males as if they were book-banning Bostonians
of another age snooping for evidence of political and moral sins.
If students could see how the old texts were tools to oppress the
weak, the deconstructionists argue, and if they could read more
politically correct texts instead, then we could construct a new
generation freed of the evils of the past.

Among these deconstructionists, or postmodernists as they are
more generally called, are some of the last true believers in Marxism left on the planet. This makes some sense, since Marxism
also holds that humans have no essential selves but are socially
constructed and therefore can be reconstructed. All human motivation, say these materialistic cynics, is tied to struggles for re-
sources and power. DWEMs, the dead white European males,
they argue, have used literature as one weapon with which to
brainwash everyone else into thinking them deserving of high
positions of status and power. Their analysis of *Moby Dick* or
Huckleberry Finn dismisses the themes of the human need to
break out of structure and instead "problematizes," "contextual-
izes," and "politicizes" them by revealing the sneaky ways in
which these books subtly and sometimes not so subtly enhance
white male dominance (or "hegemony") over others. Put all such
works together and you have "the canon," that collection of
works used for generations to brainwash America's youth. Instead
of being brainwashed by a sexist, racist canon, they argue, why
not let us who know better brainwash you instead?

Their goal, then, is to destroy this evil canon and replace it
with texts that celebrate women, blacks, Native Americans, gays,

poor people, and any of the other marginalized groups on the earth. The Holy Trinity of Race, Class, and Gender are the basic categories of oppressed persons whom these professors are struggling to free. To contextualize is not to find some real context, since none exists, but to look at the text through the lenses of one of the privileged groups. Hence, papers on *Huckleberry Finn* today heavily stress how black kids feel having to read a book with the n-word in it. Eco-critics, I presume, contextualize *Moby Dick* from the whale's point of view. Papers for such classes that understand this agenda and help push it along thus get big fat A's. A student once told me she loved her American lit class because "all I have to do is say white people oppress black people and I get an A every time."

This return from grand generalities of beauty, truth, and love to the specific acts of power embedded in the text is part of a general rejection of the grand generalities that have guided Western civilization. Those so-called meta-narratives, these critics say, are but thinly disguised myths the elite employed to bamboozle the mob. Any talk of principle, truth, justice, are, like the rules of grammar, but tools for one group's manipulating others. Just as right-to-work laws sound good but were passed to crush the unions and keep working people down, so too freedom of speech, they say, is an excuse for letting racists hurt people of color. Nor is this as far-fetched as it might seem. Ideals do tend to develop in ways that reinforce the positions of the people in power. Even revolutionary parties, like Mexico's Party of the Institutional Revolution, when institutionalized become the tools of a corrupt elite. Look at Cuba or the U.S.S.R. Noble principles do indeed get corrupted and used for ignoble ends. When the missionaries arrived in Africa, so the saying goes, the Africans had the land and the missionaries had the Bible. After a while, the missionaries had the land and the Africans had the Bible. Even religion may be but a pretext for power.

The bottom line of the deconstructionists' argument is that words have no true meaning, no presence. A sentence is only a "groundless chain of signifiers" open to infinite manipulation. Their guru, Jacques Derrida, has said that there is "nothing outside the text," at least nothing we can ever know. Words, he says, are but signifiers defined only by other words, which are themselves but words defined only by words. Hence, language is a self-referential loop that never points beyond itself. Like Luther of old, he claims that the communion wafer and wine are but symbols and not, as the priests say, the true body and blood of Christ. That the symbols are anything more than empty symbols is a lie the priests made up to serve their own worldly ends and to keep the peasants down. So we are all stuck in a verbal virtual reality only imagining that our words have any presence or true meaning. All of the great ideas, the great texts, the stirring speeches, are lying meta-narratives, tools of politics and power like the priests' claim that a cookie is really Christ.

Words thus can be manipulated by the elite creators of culture to serve their class or race or gender interests. One of the cute stunts these theorists pull is to use quotation marks excessively to try to acknowledge that though "they" "use" "words," they "understand" that "each" "word" "really" "has" "a" "multiplicity" "of" "possible" "meanings." Once upon a time, intelligent readers took it for granted that all language is full of multiple possibility; that was part of the fun of reading. Today, theorists give lectures in which their constant fingering of little quote marks in the air makes it appear they are signing. One wag has suggested that every university put up a large quotation sign on each side of campus to remind us all, I suppose, that we live in a fallen realm of uncertainty and ambiguity where the old absolutes no longer can be worshiped without doubt. These folks would have been quite at home in Puritan New England.

If no meta-narrative can be trusted, then, as Ahab asked, on what rock in this slippery world can we stand? If everything is relative and contingent, if it all depends on what the meaning of "is" is, on what basis can any belief be justified? Well, it can't. Fox Mulder is right: Trust no one. If some larger truth cannot be known and no text can be trusted, this leaves us with two options: nihilism or tribalism. Some do embrace the former, but most postmodernists seem comfortable with what they call "privileging" certain interests and arbitrarily making their empowerment the bottom line. So a gay African American woman might make the interests of her community the central planet around which the rest of the cosmos orbits. Or a Serb might make every political and moral decision rest on what is best not for mankind or freedom or any other meta-narrative but for Greater Serbia. Immigrants from Thailand or El Salvador are thus urged not to give up their particular identity in favor of the American melting-pot meta-narrative but to retain their culture. If we don't know any cosmic truths greater than ourselves, then at least we should be able to identify who our friends are. According to this school of thought, our choice is either someone else's self-serving, lying meta-narrative or "Deutschland Über Alles." Take your pick.

This was the tribalism I found in Eastern Europe, where each ethnic group sees the world only from its own narrow corner. The problem with communism, one Slovak told me, was that the party was run by Czechs. If Slovaks had been in control, it would have worked. When in 1992 I congratulated my students on their new freedom, I was told that Slovakia had been free once before, under Hitler. Slovakia was free then, I had to be told, because Hitler had put a Slovak in charge of the puppet Slovak state. My insistence that freedom meant something more than ethnic power caused them to shake their heads in pity and to tell me I was "naive." These students rejected the meta-narratives of "freedom" and "socialism"; their primary loyalty was to their tribe. Those Slovaks who wanted something more than tribalism had long since emigrated to America to join others already engaged in that naive search for some truth outside of the solipsistic subjectivity of our entrenched texts. But perhaps the cynics are right, and we have no song to sing other than "which side are you on?" The debate is a real one with powerful historical arguments on both sides.

The best that has come out of the postmodernist effort, now into its third decade, is the rediscovery of neglected works that had not been included in the standard anthologies taught to first-year college students. Today's literary anthologies overflow with poems, stories, essays, and political polemics that would be totally unfamiliar to anyone who learned American literature in the bad old days.

The worst to come out of this effort is the self-righteous assumption, seldom acknowledged, that those who point out the socially constructed nature of reality have a superior insight, as if they somehow were above the brainwashing that got to the rest of us, or—in the words of Pilgrim father William Bradford—"as if they were wiser than God." Having destroyed the old culture in the name of relativism, these elitists now imagine that they know a better substitute, and often their new rules and new codes of behavior are even more rigid than Nurse Ratched's. As Roland Barthes, one of the early deconstructionists, so blatantly revealed, "Reality is nothing but a meaning, and so can be changed to meet the needs of history when history demands the subversion of the foundations of civilization as we know it." Hence, the generation that in the name of freedom flaunted its use of the four-letter f-word in the 1960s now insists that the use of words that even sound like the six-letter n-word should be severely punished. Once they were for opening up the jails; now they are for locking all of us wretched sinners in the stocks. Condemning this loafers' paradise, they would herd us all into their workers' paradise and throw away the key.

Ironically, when today's radicals were the baby boomers of the 1960s rebelling against their parents, they did so by embracing a romantic essentialism. Nature, human and nonhuman, provided the alternative to Nurse Ratched's military-industrial combine. Because the 1950s were a period of conservative social construction, the rebellious 1960s brought forth an effort to let our essential nature all hang out. Every revolution that has ever succeeded has done so by embracing some essential belief that God, or History, is on its side and "the force" is with it. Martin Luther King Jr. was able to stand up to the racists because as a Baptist minister he felt God at his side. Malcolm Little, just another conk-haired, two-bit street punk, became Malcolm X only after finding Islam. The post-modern cynics think that by attacking essentialism and destroying any belief in the true meaning of words, they are tearing down the establishment and empowering the oppressed. They are dead wrong. They are only empowering themselves with clever word games.

They are certainly right that almost everything in culture is in a sense artificial, a con-game. But most of us have long since assumed that we are part of the brotherhood of sinners and real-

ized there is no moral Mt. Sinai on which to stand to look down
on the evil idolaters below. Most of us know, as Melville said,
that we are forced to live in the world and accept its paper
money "as if." The tribe, after all, must also be socially constructed, no more real than any meta-narrative. And Marxism is
as much a meta-narrative as any. Their solutions have no more
legitimacy than any others except to serve their elitest ends. We
need not new structures, but no structures. We need to escape
from whatever Egyptian structure oppresses us, cross the wilderness, and break on through to whatever truth exists outside our
lying texts. Only if we escape from whatever tribal collectivism is
manipulating us and try to stand alone as individual selves might
we imagine a way finally to escape ourselves. That is what it
would mean to be free, at least according to this naive dead-
white-you're-a-peein'-on-us male.

Francobabble for Freshmen

All of this interest in our perception of the text leads away from
the New Critical study of the text as a thing in itself to the opposite extreme where context and perception become everything.
Some English professors have all but given up on actually teaching literature and instead assign their students heavily theoretical philosophical discussions on perception and politics. French
postmodern theorists like Jacques Lacan, Jacques Derrida, and
Michel Foucault are among the more notorious of these Fran-
cobabblers. Students sometimes get taken in by these critics to
the point of losing all common sense.

To understand their temptation, imagine yourself gazing out a
window at a tree. A naive human being would see the tree and
appreciate its presence and even, perhaps, its beauty. But theorists would want to look not at the tree but at the lenses that dis-
tort their vision of the tree. They would have a good point. The
light on the tree changes our perception of it. At dawn and dusk,
sunlight brings out colors different from those at high noon. So
the light outside is one factor that affects our perception. So is
the content of the air between our building and the tree. The
window out of which we look is glass and has its own shades and

imperfections that prevent us from seeing the tree as it really is. If the air outside can be a medium through which our gaze passes and is warped, so too the air inside the room. Then if we are wearing glasses, these human constructions perched on our noses clearly alter our perception. But so do the lenses of our eyeballs. Finally, and perhaps most important, the expectations and assumptions built up in our brains over our lifetimes affect how we see what we only think we see. Beauty, as they rightly say, is in the mind of the beholder. An infant, Jonathan Edwards once pointed out, reaches up to touch the moon, not yet knowing it is far away; the adult has learned to see the moon as far away and no longer has the innocence the child once did. So white policemen, seeing a black man reaching for his wallet, see a criminal going for his gun. Deconstruction dissects this process of our fall from grace. It looks not at things but at the looking.

Can a male look at a female without seeing all that he knows about sex? Can a white person look at a black person, or a black person at a white person, without 400 years of racial stereotypes and grievances getting in the way? We all like to think we are free of bias, that even if we do harbor some lingering prejudices, we can by sheer exertion of will overcome them. That belief in the human will's ability to be in control of itself is the old modernist illusion. It is Robert Frost exerting his "will" or Ahab whose soul "by its own sheer inveteracy of will, forced itself against Gods and devils into a kind of self-assumed, independent being of its own." As a counterargument, the postmodernists claim we are so caught up in the constructs of a fallen world that it is naive to imagine we can ever, as Ahab put it, break through the mask and with our wills reach outside of our constructed selves. We will never, they say, walk in the garden with Reality knowing it as it really is, for the seeing self is the one constructed, and the I cannot look itself in the eye. We can never get to the beginning of the chain of cause and effect and see, as Moses did, even the backside of that First Cause that made us.

Thus, who we are affects our perception, not just of trees but of everything, including everything in works of literature. We are caught in the illusion like the people in the movie *The Matrix*

or like a *Star Trek* character lost in the holodeck. We are so en-
trapped that we have no way even to know it, and every place we
run to get away is still within this virtual-reality illusion. We are
caught in a fallen text of a world. A Reality may be out there, but
we cannot know it. We can ask what a word or a text "means."
But we would then have to step back a degree and ask, "What
does it mean to 'mean?'" And then we would have to retreat a
further step and ask, "What is the meaning of wanting to know
what the meaning of meaning means?" The regression is infinite. There is no solid ground on which to stand.

Given all this, and fascinating as it is, some people get lost in
the contemplation of the glass through which we view the world
darkly and lose all sight of the tree outside the window. Try it.
You can focus your eye on the tree outside or on the distortions
in the glass of the window, but not both. You can focus on the
room in front of you or on the sworls that swim across the lenses
of your eyes, but not both. So you can concentrate on the theory
of perception or you can read *Moby Dick*, but not both. After the
19th century Transcendentalist Margaret Fuller walked straight
into a tree, she explained, "I saw the tree but didn't realize it."
She was a theorist ahead of her time.

The best approach is, as in so much in life, to try to achieve
some balance, or failing that to tack back and forth like a sailboat
sailing into the breeze. Just as you need to balance a formal and
informal voice, the snob and the slob, the literal and the symbolic, so you need to discuss the text as if it were as it appears,
and then you also need to acknowledge the problems of your
personal perception of it. We need to look at the tree, but we
also need to be aware of ourselves looking and to watch ourselves watching ourselves watch. All that is part of the context of
the text, and we do need ultimately to be free of the texts that
control us. But don't suck too hard on the opium pipe of theory.
Otherwise, like some freak from the 1960s who dropped too
much acid, you may follow Charlie Manson down the spiral of
infinite regression into madness. We may desire some ultimate
mystic freedom from structures like government, moral codes,
paradigms, the electric grid, our very bodies and identities, but
we also need these structures to survive. Like the watcher on the

masthead in *Moby Dick*, you might drift off into these platonic dreams and forget your constructed identity. As Melville says,

> while this sleep, this dream is on ye, move your foot or hand an inch, slip your hold at all, and your identity comes back in horror. Over Descartian vortices you hover. And perhaps, at mid-day, in the fairest weather, with one half-throttled shriek you drop through that transparent air into the summer sea, no more to rise forever. Heed it well, ye Pantheists!

Morality Plays

Whatever voice you choose to write in, resist the temptation to preach. Moralism makes for lousy papers. For one thing, moral appeals tend to assume that a common sense of morality exists and that an appeal to this common morality will be effective. This assumption is unwarranted. Our most sincerely held beliefs may well be the products of our peculiar environments and not as universal as we wish to believe. If the moral posture is one that is widely accepted, then the point of the paper is quite ordinary and not a good topic. Essays on racism in these delicate times often end up as safe, sane, moralistic pronouncements about how bad hate is and how wonderful it would be if everyone could just get along and love each other. Is this an argument? Who would argue against it?

Such sappy sentimentalisms beg the important questions. Why do some people hate? What causes it? How can these causes be addressed? Can they be addressed? How is bigotry manifested? In what unconscious ways does it make itself felt? How can the heart be changed? What must we do to be saved? These are the kinds of questions that need to be asked and answered. We are all against poverty, war, and injustice, for motherhood and pesticide-free, chemically uncontaminated apple pie. Accept that and move on. If you suspect that some of us do need a little moral preaching, then the job of your paper is not to preach the word but to show us that our assumptions of innocence are unjustified. The task of making us see the beams in

our own eyes is a complex one and requires more than a moralistic finger wagging in our faces.

One graduate student in my Early American Lit seminar
thought he had said all that was to be said of the narratives of
the first explorers by arguing that these men intentionally used
the phrase "the new world" to justify stealing the land from the
Indians. He could not, however, identify the people to whom
they (or he) thought they had to justify it. No explorers in the
1500s imagined that they might have to justify taking the land
from the Indians any more than they had to justify taking it
from the wolves. Had he said that the use of the phrase unintentionally had this result, I would have credited him with a mi-
nor insight. But he had been taught that the smug unveiling of
other people's crimes is the essence of literary analysis. He did
not, however, tell us whether he was wearing leather shoes; nor
would he admit the relevance of the question. Odd, isn't it, how
people who claim there is no truth can be so certain of other
people's sins?

The tendency to turn the study of literature, or anything else
in the humanities, into a morality play of evil white men and
virtuous others should be avoided at all costs, yet not because
we white men aren't evil. We are, but so is everybody else.
Blindly privileging one group over another, even the oppressed
over their oppressors, is the root of prejudice. Many of today's
oppressors were yesterday's oppressed who still imagine themselves the underdogs. Meta-narratives have their problems, but
so does racism. Emotional appeals to reject a position because
the people who hold it are not nice are irrelevant ad hominem
attacks. Atrocities are caused on both sides of every war. Any
claim to the contrary is propaganda. Ideas need to be debated
on their merits, not on the inhumanity of the people who hold
them. Holding other human beings as property was certainly
evil, but people who own pets ought to wonder whether in 500
years students will not look back at them with the same moral
outrage.

Nor is it legitimate to assume that uncovering the motivations
behind some act or idea is all that's necessary to discredit it, as if
the only ideas worth having are somehow free of any self-inter-

est. If every effect has a cause, so too do ideas. That the person arguing for personal property rights and against conservation efforts is a lawyer for a developer should certainly make us suspicious of his arguments. But even a self-interested developer might be right. What is more, we tree-huggers who oppose development also have our self-interest at heart, no matter how well we disguise it even from ourselves. We should be equally suspicious of every point of view and examine them all carefully, not just the views of people we don't like. That's equality.

Understanding how our agenda shapes our perception is important, but if anyone's words could be dismissed for being the product of self-interest, only silence would remain. Even the revelation that some text helps keep some group in power cannot be a final word. Rationalizations constitute the fallen world we live in. Like the paper money in our wallets, they are part of the illusion and must be read and analyzed the same as everything else "as if."

Avoid also the danger of thinking an explanation of a behavior is necessarily a justification for it. Even racists have motivations that can be analyzed. A student ought to be able to write a paper explaining the causes that led James Earl Ray to shoot Martin Luther King without being accused of making excuses for him. Marvin Harris, the anthropologist, has a detailed historical explanation of why the Hindu taboo against eating beef made good ecological sense for India. But he has also found himself under attack for justifying "irrational" behavior. No human behavior is without some cause, he explains, and no one's behavior is any more irrational than that of "the average asshole on the street."

Students who first get introduced to the wonderful labyrinths of meaning behind Marxism or Hinduism or Republican economics sometimes imagine that these complex constructs must be valid because nothing else has ever been shown to them in such detail and analysis. Unfortunately, every ideology and movement in the world, from Hitler's to Stalin's to Adam Smith's, is equally complex if explored in depth. Hence, complexity alone is a wash and no proof of merit. We are all equally complex and equally crazy.

Untangling the knot of motivation is difficult if not impossible. We too often assume that discovering why a behavior happens is the end of the story. If we were all truly logical Vulcans, then perhaps once our illogical words and actions were pointed out, we might simply change. But being human, we continue with our original conditioning regardless. Freudian psychotherapists long ago gave up hope that revealing the cause of a neurosis would magically cure it. I, for instance, hate mincemeat. The very smell of it makes me shudder. And I know why. When I was seven, I laughed at something during Thanksgiving dinner and got a piece of mincemeat pie wedged up inside my nose. But knowing that today does not make me shudder any less when tortured with the smell of mincemeat. It may be possible to untangle the cause-and-effect relationships that make some people racist or anti-Semitic. But having discovered that, we still have to find a cure. Finger wagging never works.

11

The Social Sciences

What's the Dif?

Not that any huge difference exists between a paper for anthropology and one for English, but students often exaggerate the differences that do exist and cause themselves and their teachers unnecessary grief. The social sciences, by their very use of that word "science," like to imagine themselves as somehow more objective and disciplined than those wackos in the English department. The word "science" comes from the Latin *scio*, which means "I know." Science takes its claims to knowledge seriously and has little patience with the kind of relativistic solipsism that runs rampant in English departments. There is a truth and they know it. They did build that bomb, didn't they? But the hard sciences look down on the soft social sciences as much as the social sciences look down on the literary types. We thus have a continuum with the hard sciences like biology and physics on one end, the relativists in the English department on the other end, and the many branches of the social sciences defensively in the middle.

"Real" Marxists from the sociology or economics department can barely break bread with their literary cousins across the hall. And all of the social sciences believe their work to be based in strict adherence to certain methodological principles and their precise terminology. Partly because of this sneer, the professors in the English department adopted French postmodern theory so that they too could have certain methodological principles and an incomprehensible vocabulary to go with them. In the end, the two groups all roughly do pretty much the same thing in the same way, alas.

Students still have to deal with those perceptions. Therefore, a paper for sociology or anthropology needs to adopt science's arrogant "we know," that assumption of a common body of knowledge backed up by scholarly studies. You can make almost any claim you want if you can find a journal article somewhere, or a scholarly book, that can be footnoted as a reference for your "fact." You need to spell out carefully near the beginning of the paper which or whose methodology the paper is based upon. And you absolutely must have studies from reputable journals to back up any claims. Subjective color is appropriate in an English paper, but a social science paper also requires a vigorous and engaging voice. Use anecdotes as you would analogies to illustrate your points, but do not depend upon them to substantiate your points. The crucial difference is that a paper for a social science class must state its objectives clearly and use evidence that will stand up to critical scrutiny. In short, cover your ass.

Statistics are also important. They are the data upon which the paper's generalities are based. No human trait is absolute, so generalities are a necessary evil. We look for generalities but distrusting them. Hence, a study of any group of people has to determine at what point the repetition of a certain trait becomes "statistically significant." If one out of five African Americans is lactose intolerant, is that significant? Or must the statistic be three out of five before we start making generalities about whether African Americans have difficulty digesting milk? Such statistical questions need to be addressed as part of the discussion of methodology. Another similarity between the social sciences and the hard sciences is their reliance upon the importance of verifying a thesis by making predictions and then being able to have those predictions come true. If the spread of gonorrhea is tied to the availability of inexpensive beer, then a study comparing the spread of the disease with the rates of taxation of beer ought to show a statistically significant correlation between the two, with the rate of gonorrhea going up if the tax goes down and down if the tax goes up. Once a prediction like this is made, proposals can be written, grant money secured, the study conducted, and the results analyzed and published. Such a study was actually done by the Centers for Disease Control and Prevention covering all the states from 1981 to 1995. It showed that raising the tax on a 6-pack by 20 cents could reduce gonorrhea by as much as 9%. Until the beer companies can fund a new study contradicting this one, this thesis stands.

One major difference between the humanities and the sciences is that the humanities celebrate the lone individual who comes up with fresh new insights, whereas the sciences celebrate the collective accumulation of knowledge. In the sciences, you need to show you have a grasp of the past work done on your subject. In this, the sciences can be thought of as Catholic and the humanities as Protestant. The Catholics, like grammar snobs, believe in the importance of obedience to rules passed down through a hierarchical structure; the Protestants tend to be slobs who emphasize each individual's responsibility to recreate the world for himself or herself.

The social sciences are not only sciences; they are also social. That is, they deal with the slippery problems of human behavior. For this reason the so-called hard sciences like chemistry and physics and biology think the social sciences, including economics and "business science," are no more real science than literary theory is. All of this of course means that jostling for status plays a key role in all these academic battles. At least within the humanities, which in my opinion includes literary and social sciences, and the arts, each discipline uses a different language but pretty much says the same stuff. The job for the hardworking student is to learn the languages of the different departments. At bottom, most American colleges are simply language schools, and the job of the student is to master several different professional tongues.

Free to Be? Free at All?

The first problem any student entering any of these disciplines must deal with is the bugaboo of free will. There ain't no such thing. I have mentioned this before, and from past experience I know that few of you believe me. Therein lies your first mistake. To be sure, our popular culture worships free will as the cornerstone of liberty. Our legal system enshrines it as the basis of our law. Our preachers tend to finesse the issue by saying God gave us free will; don't try to define it and don't ask how. But our academics have long since abandoned the notion as quaint in the extreme. This causes a great deal of trouble, especially in court. There the prosecutor argues that an accused mass murderer is a responsible free agent and should be punished for his crimes, but the defense attorney brings in social scientists who argue that the poor man is a victim who, given all that he has suffered, did not have any control over the circumstances that shaped him into the murderer he has become. He is in fact not evil but sick and suffering from a syndrome. We all have our favorite examples of this. Mine is a high school principal in Fairfax, Virginia, who claimed in court that he was suffering from a "psychosexual disorder" that made him unable to supervise women without trying to force them to have sex with him. The courts were suspicious of that line, but he scored with the Virginia Retirement System, which awarded him a disability retirement of $38,000 a year because his "disorder" prevented him from finding employment in his field.

Because we are all shaped by our environment, a clever defense lawyer can construe any act as the product of a syndrome. And he would be right. We are each the combined set of all our syndromes. I suffer from tmfp, a serious too-many-freshman-papers syndrome that drives me into pds, or punish-the-dumb-student, syndrome when I am unable to alleviate the symptoms with my occasional ale-does-more-than-Milton-can-to-justify-God's-ways-to-man syndrome.

That we are free to do whatever we want is not the issue. The issue is why do we want what we want. This is why I ask my students what their favorite ice cream is and why. Our likes and dislikes are in us when we come to make decisions; we choose what is already programmed in us to want. If our desire for ice cream is stronger, we order the double chocolate fudge; if our desire to be thin is stronger than our desire for the ice cream, we pass on by. But which desire is stronger is not something we can control. We can only respond. In every decision we make, some prior inclination leads. Nor is this a recent or a leftist idea. Jonathan Edwards said over 200 years ago we no more create the thoughts that come into our minds than we create the sights that come into our eyes or the noises that come into our ears, but for some reason we are blessed with the illusion that we are in control. As Ishmael says in *Moby Dick*, "Now that I recall all the circumstances, I think I can see a little into the springs and motives which being cunningly presented to me under various disguises, induced me to set about performing the part I did, besides cajoling me into the delusion that it was a choice resulting from my own unbiased free will and discriminating judgment."

We live in a cause-and-effect world in which every effect has a prior cause. Try to imagine someone choosing his prior desire. Suppose you like chocolate ice cream. Could you change that to vanilla? The very wanting to change must come first. And if you really want to change your wanting, the deed already was done and not by your "free will." We imagine, like Ishmael, that our own discriminating judgment is at the core of our consciousness, but reality seems to say we do not create our own priorities.

If we don't have free will, then can we really be free? The Communists during the cold war argued that we Americans only imagine we are free, that we are brainwashed into believing this. What is more, the very forces that brainwash us into believing we are free also control our every desire. Americans, they say, are so bombarded by advertising and other manipulative techniques that we are in fact all puppets of capitalism. B. F. Skinner, the father of American behaviorism, wrote a scandalous book titled *Beyond Freedom and Dignity*, which following on his famous *Walden II*, argued that freedom is an illusion and we would all be better off if society were arranged by behavioral scientists so that the conditioning that is the inevitable source of our thoughts and feelings would be a product of central planning rather than the random chaos we enjoy now. Here, perhaps, is a clue as to why so many social scientists are Marxists. If we are each socially constructed, then freedom truly is a myth. Since we are all brainwashed anyway, why not let the over-educated experts who know best do it right?

Nature and Nurture

Once the idea is at least being chewed on that we are not in control of our own thoughts, the next question is, "All right, where do our thoughts come from?" If we are as programmed as a bee crossing a cow pasture, where did this programming originate? Here we have two choices: The programming is either innate and we are born with it as a gift from the universe, or it is a product of our experiences interacting with our environment. The debate between the essentialists and the social constructionists therefore turns out to be but another version of the great, eternal debate between nature and nurture. Here is where the fun begins.

Despite what your freshman sociology professor might have told you, the debate between nature and nurture has not been settled. In the 1950s, when white male pigs were in charge, the prevailing notion was that human beings are shaped by natural urges over which we must exercise control. It was an era in which people believed in nature's power but tried to resist it, seeing it as evil. Among other things, the experience of World War II had taught Americans that under the thin surface of self-control and rationality, human beings were raging beasts. It was a lesson not soon forgotten. Human society, they said, must exercise the discipline to train people to be civilized.

But the children of that generation, raised in comfort in suburbia, forgot the lesson and turned on the structures of society with which their parents had hoped to keep the irrational under control. To us baby boomers, the rules were not keeping us from evil but reinforcing the evils of segregation, racism, and war. We boomers of the 1960s embraced nature as a force for good rather than as a monster to be restrained under lock and key. The civil rights movement, freeing black Americans from repression, can be seen as a product of this process. If, as James Baldwin said to many whites, black Americans symbolize the primitive emotions of the self, it makes sense that the 1950s snobs would want to repress them and the 1960s slobs would want to set them free. Where our parents had tried to tuck it all in, we baby boomers let it all hang out.

Since then, a major shift has taken place. The heirs of the 1960s, unable to create a social revolution simply by letting it all hang out, have abandoned their romantic faith in nature and turned to their old enemy, nurture, to finish the social revolution. The emphasis changed from how nature can save us from the nurture that warped us to how social engineering can set us right.

Old hippies who once believed in freedom now sit on academic committees hammering out complex rules for how people should behave on dates and what words are too dirty to be spoken, written, or thought. Nurse Ratched is now a member of NOW. The feminist movement, in particular, has had to fight against the idea that women are somehow submissive and weak and emotional by nature. Black people have had to fight against the racist notion that African Americans are intellectually inferior or lazy by nature. The struggle for social justice and equality has led to a dogmatic insistence that human beings are not products of nature but are shaped by their environment. A feminist once argued with me that even birds do not inherit the ability to build nests and fly south but somehow learn these things from their parents. It was an extreme example, but it was a good indicator of the trend.

In the 1980s, sociobiologists like Edward Wilson began to challenge the prevailing paradigm and to argue that human nature owes more to nature than to nurture. Since then, a host of new studies have argued, using data and all the rest, that nature after all really is in control and nurture but the icing on the cake. B. F. Skinner defines those natural factors that shape our species as "contingencies of survival" and those more recent factors that shape our individual personalities as "contingencies of reinforcement." Evolutionary psychologists argue that a middle ground exists between hardwired nature and social construction. They, like cultural anthropologists, see much of our behavior as having been shaped by the long human experience in Africa before civilization began. To them, our nature is part of our inheritance but is something that can change over time. The dilemma is in trying to figure out where to draw any lines. Denounced as racists and sexists by the social constructionists, these folks have had to shout loudly, but they have been heard.

So today, at the beginning of the new millennium, we are back where we always were, in a debate with two sides well matched and well armed. Do not therefore let anyone tell you that one side or the other has been proved right. An argument exists here, one you can exploit to your benefit in any paper you need to write. We are almost certainly shaped neither by nature nor by nurture solely but by the complex interaction of both. Where to draw the line is one of the first questions to ask. Think of an oak tree growing in the desert. It is still an oak tree with many of the natural characteristics of an oak, but because of its environment, it will not look like its cousins in Ohio.

If you are convinced that either nature or nurture is the chief cause of whatever trait you are writing about, then the problem becomes one of identifying those factors in the environment or in the genes that make us who we are. Remember the bottom-line question: What makes people tick? In some ways, a good social science paper is little more than gossip with footnotes.

Praise and Blame

One of the most stubborn denials of the validity of any form of determinism, whether essential or social, comes with the need to believe that people can and should be held responsible for their acts. That horny high school principal in Fairfax, Virginia, needs to take responsibility for his acts and not blame them on some "psychosexual disorder." On that, I think even the feminists would agree. But doesn't an insistence on determinism eliminate personal responsibility? How can we call people "bad" and throw them in jail if they are not at fault? During the 1992 Los Angeles riots, after a mob dragged a white truck driver from his cab and beat him, apologists argued that the rioters were victims of "mob hysteria" that overcame their normal thinking thus mitigating their blame. Cooler heads pointed out that such excuses might also be made for white mobs that lynched blacks. Recently, a white ball player was forced to undergo psychological treatment for making racist remarks on television. Even racism is now a syndrome. How can anyone be held responsible for any evil deed?

Think of a pit bull raised from a puppy in the dark in a cellar, fed only every other day and beaten with a stick at every opportunity. The dog will grow up mean, and if it escapes some day, it will attack the first person it runs into. Is the dog's behavior its fault? Yes and no. It did not cause its own anger; nor can it be expected to control it. But it is still a "bad" dog, however that meanness got programmed into it. The very word "fault" suggests why we get so confused over this issue. The word also means a crack in the earth, or a vase. If something is wrong with an item, we say it has a "fault." Literally, the crack is the vase's fault. The vase may not have caused the crack, but the fault is there nonetheless. We human beings all have faults we did not cause. They are our faults. And like the pit bull, we can be restrained and imprisoned for our faults "as if" we were responsible. Like the Fairfax principal and the pit bull, we can be separated from society and locked up, even forced to undergo reprogramming. But the principal, like the pit bull, also deserves our sympathy. "There but for the grace of God go I" is a moral stance superior to "Throw all the evil people in jail so the world will be safe for us good guys." As Edwards said, being aware of our mutual contingency ought to make us all more tolerant.

Cause and Effect Again

An Englishman once traveling in India asked his native guide one evening what he thought the world was. "Ah, Sahib," replied the Indian, "the world is a great elephant and we live on its back."

"What then holds up this elephant?" asked the Englishman.

"It stands on the back of a big turtle," came the reply.

"And what holds up that turtle?"

"It stands on the back of another turtle."

"But what then does that turtle stand on?"

"Ah, Sahib," came the answer, "after that it is turtles all the way down."

The story is remembered and retold because it is a metaphor for the infinite regression we get not only in trying to watch ourselves watching, but also in trying to decide which came first, the chicken or the egg. The social science paper is thus an exercise, as is the literary paper, in trying to push back the mystery as far as possible. If we are to argue for the need for more battered women's shelters in the Bronx, we must explain why women in the Bronx are battered and why we think funding shelters will have the desired effect. But every cause is itself the effect of some prior cause. Behind each of these is an infinite regression of whys.

The biggest danger is in taking this responsibility too lightly and assuming that we know the turtle at the bottom of the pile. We don't. Reality is far too complex. As Thomas Hooker once said, "Our cockleshells will never comprehend that sea." Easy answers must always be challenged with another "why?" Any dogmatist who thinks he or she knows any answers needs to think again.

A recent study establishing that African American males have much higher death rates than other American males elicited, when it was published, the predictable responses. Here, once again, was evidence of the racist nature of American society. Further analysis, however, revealed that greater differences existed between different groups of black males than between black and white males and that poor white males in the deep South had roughly the same death rates as blacks. The conclusion was that "persistent aspects of the lifestyle of the south" affected black American males whose families came north but continued to eat a heart-clogging diet of greasy pork and fried chicken just like their redneck neighbors. The first responses fit a preconception but turned out to be prejudging the case.

We see the same problem in the debate over global warming. Scientific statistics certainly seem to show a persistent warming of the climate over the past thirty years. And scientists have determined that carbon dioxide in the atmosphere, such as that from pollution, might cause the climate to get warmer. But the cause-and-effect relationship has never been proved, only assumed and generally by those who are looking for arguments to cut down on pollution anyway. Historians identify what they call a "little ice age" running roughly from 1400 to 1850 during which the planet was a lot cooler than it had been in the year 1000 when Greenland was green. We may in fact be going through some larger climate changes that have little if anything to do with our pollution. Not everything is our fault. We may not be that powerful.

Scientists like to pretend they are objective, but in fact they are no more objective than anyone else. The famous "search for truth" is more often than not a search for evidence to back up a favorite thesis. But even so, we have to confront a report on oil pollution paid for by Exxon by analyzing its evidence and logic.

Right and wrong, true and false, are subjective even in the sciences. The scholar who brings the most evidence and the best logic to the debate wins regardless of motivation or who paid her bills. We must be aware of bias, but we still must live in the world "as if."

The job, then, of a social science paper is to push back the chain of cause and effect in order to discover all the factors that manipulate us. No professor expects his or her students to trace everything back to some First Cause, but it is important to realize that we are all caught in the many chains of cause and effect and to try our best to reveal them. Only mystics and romantics believe we can ever break out of these chains; social scientists are practical sorts who accept the world as given and try to understand it so that we can make the best of our cages.

Those who think they know the name of that First Cause are dogmatists who have left the objective skepticism of science for some political or religious cause. The many schools of analysis can be thought of as the products of differing answers to this question. Marxists believe that competition for material goods is at the core of it all. Feminists see the First Cause in gender relationships. Freudians are convinced that sex is behind our every move. Astrologers blame it on the movements of the planets. "Men either worship the true God or some idol," Jonathan Edwards explained. "Something will have the heart of man, and that which a man gives his heart to may be called his God." It may be, as Edwards and the deconstructionists say, that objectivity does not exist. But the sciences, including the social sciences, try at least to maintain an objective stance, to use facts and statistics, and to keep themselves open to any possibility.

Constructed Snobs and Essential Slobs

Return for a moment to the discussion of picking a topic: Note that whether you are writing a paper for English class or for sociology, you can find a pattern that runs through all of this by looking for the comparisons and contrasts. On one side is Nurse Ratched, a social constructionist if there ever was one, trying to reshape the broken products of society so that they can fit back in and be productive citizens. She undoubtedly is a stickler for good grammar too, a true snob who believes in structure. On the other side, we have Randle McMurphy celebrating his sexist, racist self without any concern for the consequences of his words and actions. He is an uneducated, antisocial essentialist who accepts himself as natural. His liberation from the mental hospital is the escape of the free soul from its constructed cage.

Anyone who has tried to walk around some of the mentally unstable people who live on the sidewalks of New York knows that the policy of opening up the mental wards and letting the inmates run free did not do either them or society much good. Yet we are a culture that celebrates individual freedom. We do not believe that anybody ought to be brainwashed by the state, but neither do we want teenagers who have been brainwashed by video games to shoot up their high school classmates. We want people to be moral without having to enforce the rules that would make them moral. We teachers want students both to be themselves and to follow our directions. We want both structure and freedom.

In any work of literature, or any other text, we can find this conflict between the need for structure and the desire to be free. When Huckleberry Finn begins to feel lonely out there on the river, he looks for security and structure in the families and small towns along the shore until they get too oppressive. He then has to run back to the natural river, and to Jim, where he can feel free and easy, until the loneliness gets to him again. At the end of the novel, he is offered a true home with people who love him, but the last line of the book is his determination not to let himself get civilized but to light out for the territory. Similarly, Thelma and Louise escape from the structure of their dreary lives and become outlaws until they are faced with a choice between the ultimate structure of prison or the ultimate liberation of death. They too light out for the territory. Similarly, many of the issues in the social sciences, in government and politics, deal with this tension between our need for community and our desire for individual freedom. Even literary theory, with its desire to escape the shackles of imposed meanings and tyrannical texts, has a bit of *Huck Finn* in it. But it also has more than a bit of the Widow Douglas trying to impose a new moral order on the deconstructed remains of the old.

Rules and structure offer us stability, even if it is an artificial stability manipulated by elites. The alternative is the search for some essential authenticity either in the chaotic depths of the individual self or in the wilderness of nature. Thus, escape from the collective structure to the imperatives of the self leads to anarchy, which in time tends to be replaced by tyranny, and so the cycle begins again.

If you can stand back from the details and try to get a sense of the larger patterns, you may, even in the most unexpected places, find familiar themes you can write about with passion.

12

Grammatical Horrors

The symbols used here are my own and are not in universal use, at least not yet. I prefer not to use many of the standard names and phrases because I fear that too many students get lost in memorizing nomenclature and never spend enough time worrying about why these errors are forbidden. To understand the rules that govern grammar is more important than to know one hundred different phrases for various mistakes. Therefore, I have tried to find new ways of identifying common errors so that students will know why I think they are wrong.

ONW—Omit Needless Words

Taken from Strunk and White's famous *Elements of Style*, this simple rule applies more often than any other to papers I correct. I need to get a stamp made with this on it. I follow Ray Kroc's rule, "K.I.S.S.," "Keep It Simple, Stupid." The fewer words in which something can be said, the better. Don't use eight words when two will do. Don't say "Following is the next argument to be made in support of the proposition here under consideration"; say "Next, . . ." When you begin a sentence, state the subject only once (sportscasters notwithstanding): "The author of this book, he is really a jerk" should instead be "The author of this book is a jerk." Better yet, name him and the book: "In the book *Moby Dick*, by the writer Herman Melville, the author says" can easily be shortened to "In *Moby Dick*, Herman Melville writes."

NAS—Not a Sentence

A sentence must have at least a subject and a verb and usually but not always an object. Sometimes phrases will appear that do not have a subject or a verb. Like this one. Such phrases set off as if they were sentences that could stand alone are called sentence fragments or "dependent" (as opposed to "independent") clauses. More often than not, these sentence fragments will be descriptive phrases tacked to the end of sentences. They really should be preceded by a comma and not treated as a separate sentence. Never mind what *Time* does; *Time* is wrong. You can be creative later. But you must learn how to do it right before you can appreciate the liberties involved in doing it wrong. Make sure each sentence has a subject and a verb, at the very least.

MM—Misplaced Modifier

A misplaced modifier is what some grammar books call a "dangling modifier" or a "dangling participle." Whether you intend it or not, a descriptive phrase at the beginning of a sentence modifies the very first noun that follows. Hence, if you write "Walking down the street, a piano fell on my head," you are saying that a piano was walking down the street. I once read on a paper the sentence "Being the early sixties, democracy was not yet known in New Jersey." According to this sentence, democracy is "the early sixties." The sentence is weird enough without that misplaced modifier.

I also have in my overflowing file of grammatical horrors this ad for Wendy's: "As our valued guest, we guarantee to serve you" the best. In this sentence, "we" are our own "valued guest." If Wendy's wants to serve itself, it should at least make the word "guest" plural to agree with the plural "we." These mistakes abound. The sentence "Beautiful and sensually dressed, the men noticed her immediately" could make sense only if the men were at a transvestite ball. I once had to pull the car to the side of the highway and stop to jot down this one from the radio: "If not caught in time, Dr. Evans said the virus will spread." Poor Dr.

Evans, chased all over town. In my overflowing file cabinet of news clippings is a quote from the Christian Coalition chief in Iowa, Bobbie Gobel, after she was fired. She denied she had fallen from the Lord after putting her "large breast" in a parishioner's face. She was fired, she said, for being too hard on presidential candidate Steve Forbes. In response to this charge she declared, "As a Christian, God allows me to be a fruit inspector." Perhaps if God had been a Muslim, he would have told her to keep her hands off the fruit.

The MM is a mistake that readers of *The New Yorker* and other language snobs love to snicker at. If you do not want to look ridiculous, avoid misplaced modifiers.

//—Parallelism Problem

Perhaps due to its Germanic origins, English demands order. It loves consistency, symmetry, parallel structure. Things in a series must all be in the same form. Do not say "I love swimming, jogging, and sex." In this example, "sex" is not the same verb form as "swimming" and "jogging." Say "having sex." Or change the first two verbs: "I love to swim, to jog, and to . . . " (you choose your own verb here). If you are using the plural, stay with the plural. If you are in the past, stay there. If you have to change to the present, indicate clearly that you are doing so, perhaps with a new paragraph. Remember to be consistent. This is a style rule as well as a grammar rule. The most eloquent English uses parallel structures and forms to communicate. Striving to be a good writer, striving to learn how to argue effectively, means striving to use those models that enhance clear communication. I love Richard Niebuhr's description of the dismal state of Christianity in nineteenth-century America when "a God without wrath brought men without sin into a kingdom without judgment through the ministrations of a Christ without a cross."

This principle can be extended to cover those other errors of number and person that are far too common. If you begin with the first or second or third person as your subject, stick with it. Never write, "If one looks their best, you will always get laid." If you have a singular subject, use a singular verb. Note that "everyone," "anyone," "no one," "neither," are in fact singular and take singular verbs: "Everyone in this class is [not are] in danger of flunking." The committee is . . . but the members of the committee are . . . All you need do to get these right is to pay attention to the meaning of the words. Though it does not always seem so, the rules of American English are occasionally guided by logic. Curiously, British English gives the collective noun a plural verb: "The English team are playing in France this weekend." But the Brits have been going downhill since Cromwell.

Subject-verb agreement exhibits one of the irrational aspects of English usage that you simply have to accept. A clever Cambodian student, fresh off the boat, had a hard time making plurals. In his native language, "ten dog" clearly indicated that there was more than one dog. He didn't see the need for the "s" after dog to indicate more than one. "Just do it," I said. He did. When we got to verbs, he put his logical computer-nerd foot down. "Why do you put an s after the verb if the subject is singular?" he cunningly asked. "Why 'he shoots,' but 'they shoot'? Shouldn't the plural subject be indicated with an 's' and not the singular? Shouldn't it be 'he shoot' and 'they shoots'?" Logically, what he said made sense. Ever reasonable, sensitive, and full of compassion, "Just do it," I said.

A ≠ They

Getting pronouns to agree with their nouns seems to be one of the hardest English writing skills to learn. All day long you can read and hear people say, "Everyone likes their cocoa with a shot of booze." But "everyone" is a one, and "their" refers to more than one. Everyone likes his, or his and her, not their (cocoa or whatever). Do not say, "A person likes their hair to be clean." A ≠ they. I heard an ad on TV one day in which the announcer said in a very serious voice, "Once every six seconds a GM owner puts their stamp of approval on a new car." Stamp out that ad agency. Here is a quotation from a high school teacher commenting on a deadly car wreck: "I never had a student who totaled a car when they were alone." She was not, I pray, an English teacher.

AWK—Awkward

We paper graders use AWK when a sentence is so confusing that we cannot or do not have the time or patience to try to straighten it out. If you cannot tell that something sounds wrong, read the sentence out loud or have someone else read it to you. Most native English speakers will recognize when something is wrong. It is usually better to start all over again with such sentences than to try to straighten them out. Sometimes if a sentence seems truly hopeless, the best and easiest cure is to put it out of its misery. They shoot horses, don't they?

OOG—One Step Beyond AWK

"OOG" is an unpleasant gut reaction to a combination of disastrous AWKs.

BB—Back-to-Back

These errors are rare. Most college writers have learned to avoid them, but they do appear on occasion. They involve placing the same words or phrases at the end of one sentence and the beginning of the next. Clearly, when this occurs, there is some way to combine the two sentences smoothly into one. Hence, BB errors are a subset of ONW. Example: "I saw the dog. The dog was running away." Easily fixed: "I saw the dog running away."

Typo—Typographical Error

It isn't necessary for me to say that typos are to be avoided. You know that. But it is necessary for me to stress the importance of proofreading your paper before you hand it in. The reason is as much political as grammatical. A paper you did not bother to proofread even once for obvious mistakes is clearly one you don't care about. And if you don't care about it, why should I? On the other hand, a typo corrected by pen, however messy, at least shows you cared enough to look for errors and correct them. If many such corrections turn the page into visual chaos, perhaps you should seriously consider retyping that page.

Word processing introduces its own dangers. For example, even using a spell-check program does not tell you if you spelled "your" as "you" or "sea" as "see." Most programs cannot tell if in erasing some mistake you accidentally left in three words of the original sentence. Do not rely on technology to do your scud-busting for you. You must reread every blessed word yourself carefully. Typos are like rocks in a New England garden. No matter how many you find and remove, the next time you look a big one will be staring you in the face. Nevertheless, keep looking and find as many as you can.

SP—Spelling

What can I say about spelling except "Get it right!"

Poor Dan Quayle will forever serve, whatever else he does, as an example of the ridicule that might someday be heaped upon you too if you never learn to spell "potatoes."

As one of the worst spellers in Christiandom, I warn my students not to relax therefore but to worry more, for if even I recognize a misspelling on their papers, they are really in trouble. Nothing makes you look stupider than not knowing how to spell. Many common mistakes need to be dealt with individually, and the grammar handbooks often list pages of these. Remember, for instance, that there is "a rat" in "separate." You will then be less tempted to spell the word "seperate." Beware of depending upon spell checkers. They cannot sea misspellings that our other words and thus can't save you're hide.

WW—Wrong Word

Students all too often do not know what they are saying, literally. They use the wrong word and make themselves look even sillier than they are. If you are writing about a fraternity that will not accept black members, be sure not to spell it "except." To accept is to include; to except is to exclude. They sound the same but mean the opposite. Likewise, to be "a part" is to be included; to be "apart" is to be separated. "Conscience" and "conscious" are not interchangeable spellings of the same word. I could go on, but time and space are finite.

Beware also of malapropisms, words that sound right but are slightly off. These can be clever if intentional, but we teachers cannot always tell that, and we rarely give you the benefit of the doubt. The word refers to Mrs. Malaprop, a character in a play by Richard Sheridan, who kept using the wrong word to hilarious effect. It is important to know the right word and not guess at one that merely sounds close to it. Otherwise, you can appear ridiculous. Recently, a student wrote on a paper that he felt like "a pond on a chest board." I couldn't tell if he had the right image in mind and could not spell, or whether he merely had heard the phrase "pawn on a chess board" and had some idea what it meant as a generality but no idea what specific image it referred to. Then there was the reference to the "close nit family," but nits are the eggs, not the lice, so I wonder about that clan. Another student spelled hypocrisy "hippocracy." I defined that as government by hippos. Another student wrote of some people "conjugating" in the corner of the room. She meant "congregating," I think. Recently a Republican congressman from Florida put out a press release attacking Clinton for "cow towing to Cuba" in the Elian Gonzalez affair. The image of the president towing a cow across the Florida straits is bizarre, even for Clinton. I once received a paper on Malcolm X in which the student said Malcolm X was angry and eloquent "because of the manor in which he was raised" and was discriminated against "for the soul reason of race." The class howled; the student, although unnamed, blushed and slunk under his chair. Don't let it happen to you.

With the decline of literacy and the dominance of television and cinema, fewer and fewer students come to college having read more than a few assigned books. Hence, this kind of mistake is becoming increasingly common. If you do not know for sure what you are saying, take the time to look it up. That is what dictionaries are for. If you don't know anyone who owns a dictionary, you can find one on the Net.

Added to this collection should be unintended double entendres, and not limited to the risqué type either. Make sure that what you are writing cannot easily be read in some other way. I say "easily" because every teacher knows no way exists to write an exam question that some poor befuddled student won't completely misread. The hope is to avoid as much confusion as possible. I have, for instance, a legal pamphlet that calls on "All Criminal Practitioners" to attend a lecture on the practice of criminal law. An antilitter and antismoking memo passed out by my school instructed students: "Keep your butts off the sidewalks and other places where people can see them." A student once brought me a leaflet stuck under her apartment door notifying her of an upcoming insect extermination program with the sentence "Each individual will be exterminated on your floor in rotation."

13

Some Common
Stupid Mistakes

We all make mistakes, God knows. I misspelled my graduate-thesis adviser's name on every sheet of my thesis proposal. Nevertheless, such mistakes are to be avoided if possible. Here are some of the most common ones I encounter in papers from freshman comp to graduate seminars.

Its, It's, and Its'

This one is pretty simple once someone points it out to you. Here is the exception to the rule in English about how we make possessives and contractions. We usually make the possessive by adding apostrophe (') s. We make a contraction in the same way. Hence, you would think "it is" and "of it" should both be "it's." But this way confusion lies. So once upon a time someone arbitrarily decided that "it is" has priority and deserves the honor of the apostrophe. "Of it" must therefore be satisfied to live without one. So think of meaning and remember:

it is = it's   of it = its

As for "its'," a construction I have indeed seen, try to imagine the sentence that would need a possessive of the plural "its." For the only one I can imagine, the word "its" would have to appear several times on the blackboard in green chalk, and someone would have to be saying something about the many "its" and "the its' color." Other than in that ludicrous stretch, no such word exists.

The Possessive

As long as we are on the topic of apostrophes, let's deal with the possessive. Everyone knows how to make the possessive, but not everyone knows how to distinguish the plural from the singular. It's very easy. If the thing or things being possessed are being possessed by more than one thing, and the corresponding noun has an "s" at the end, the apostrophe goes outside the "s." A student who writes about "my fathers' face" is saying literally that he or she has more than one father and all those fathers share one face. Since most humans can have only one father, it should be "my father's face," or perhaps if the father is the two-faced type, "my father's faces."

Dealing with the plural possessive can get tricky when the singular form of the word ends in "s." If there is only one syllable, simply treat the word as you would any other: "my boss's foot." With two or more syllables, you have problems. And here we reach the horizon of the known world. Beyond this point, truth belongs to the person with the best argument. There is no absolute. For every expert who claims authority for a particular answer, there are two other equally valid authorities with different answers. (I was criticized at my doctoral-thesis defense because I had written repeatedly about "Jonathan Edwards' theology." Luckily, I was—oddly for me—prepared with a citation from some obscure grammar book that said if the emphasis is on the first syllable, the final "s" of the possessive could be omitted. But it was close.)

A more obscure but equally noteworthy mistake is the use of the possessive apostrophe within a possessive. It is hard to resist the temptation to write "That was a mighty wonderful speech of Churchill's." Well, the possessive is already there in the "of." To what does the "'s" refer? A noun is missing: "of Churchill's maid"? "of Churchill's dog"? We will never know. If you can't say, "That was a wonderful speech of Churchill" (and that certainly isn't idiomatic), say, "That was a wonderful speech Churchill gave." Sometimes, a writer has to go back and straighten out an entire sentence in order to fix a small problem.

The Split Infinitive

Here we separate the true language snobs from the language slobs. It is important to realize that grammar is by and large an arbitrary convention. Moses did not bring it down from Sinai. It changes constantly, especially in America. There is no board of official grammarians in this country that sits and decides the rules. These evolve through usage. What one person sees as a mistake might be seen by another as the cutting edge of change. The important thing is not to learn the rules but to learn the arguments. Second-rate minds know all the rules but only the rules; first-rate minds know all the rules and all the objections to them. If your grader in English class has a second-rate mind, it is up to you to decide how you are going to react. Either you rigidly follow his rules, or you prepare your first-rate mind to point out the problems after he hands you back your D. Understand that we graders cannot tell the difference between a clever innovation consciously contrived and a stupid mistake blundered into, and it is our duty to deny the student the benefit of the doubt. It is the student's duty to communicate his or her knowledge to us.

Nowhere does the arbitrary nature of the grammar wars surface more clearly than in disputes over the split infinitive. All of you, I trust, recognize this error. An infinitive is the "to" plus a verb, to go, to swim, to cheat, to steal, and the like. The traditional language-snob law demands that no words ever be inserted between the "to" and the verb. To do so is to split the infinitive. Yet infinitives are split all the time. What is the mission of the starship *Enterprise?* "To boldly go where no man has gone before," and to boldly split infinitives where no infinitive has been split before. The writers did change the wording in the new series, you will be glad to note. The new mission is "to boldly go where no one has gone before." The only change is a clear indicator of modern sensitivity to sexist language; "man" has been changed to "one," but the split infinitive remains. In the bold new world of the future, split infinitives are okay, but sexism is a sin.

During the Monica Lewinsky mess, I published a letter (reprinted here) in the *Washington Post* questioning the editors' front-page headline "Clinton Vows To Never Resign." I merely wanted to know if the *Post*'s editors had abandoned their style-book's warning against the split infinitive. The only answer I received was a headline, also on the front page, a short time later that read, "CIA Unable to Precisely Track Testing." At about the same time, word came down that even the editors of the prestigious *Oxford English Dictionary* had determined that the split-infinitive rule was no longer one to be taken seriously. Score another victory for the slobs.

I personally do not care if an infinitive is split as long as the meaning is clear. I force composition students to follow the old law exactly, in the hope that in the future when they do split infinitives, they will feel a twinge of shame. If they must do it, I want them at least to intentionally split (*sic*) the infinitive and not do it by accident or from ignorance. In my general literature classes, I allow split infinitives to go unpunished as long as there is not more than one word in the split. Hence, I am neither slob nor snob but wishy-washily in the middle. In no case is it okay to accidentally or intentionally split an infinitive with more than one word.

"Hopefully" and Other Controversies

As long as we are in the realm of the language snob, the other taboo besides the split infinitive that causes these folks to foam at the mouth is the misuse of the adverb "hopefully." The problem here is an interesting one. The protectors of the language fear that misuse of words ruins those words for everyone. And they are right. Just as the misuse of any liberty eventually leads to the loss of that liberty for us all, so the misuse of words leads to the destruction of our common literary heritage. Sometimes this does not matter. Sometimes it does. I personally regret the loss of "disinterested" as a word. It used to be a positive word

Notorious Split

Ever since your notorious headline "Clinton Vows to 'Never' Resign [front page, Feb. 7] I have waited for the flood of letters and the abject apology in the Ombudsman column for printing such a glaring split infinitive, not just in the body of some lengthy flood of text on an inside page, but at the very top of the front page in inch-high letters, where any impressionable child can see it.

Does the publication of this once-forbidden error signal an acceptance on the part of your paper? Does the lack of angry letters echo that concurrence on the part of your readers? If so, this is a moment in the evolution (or devolution) of the American tongue. The whole split-infinitive rule always has been a bit ridiculous, depending as it does on the archaic fact that the infinitive in Latin was one word and thus not splittable. But English teachers and defenders of the grammatical faith have been perpetuating for generations the insistence that this rule be followed.

If in fact the nation's leading newspaper, and its powerful readership, have concluded that the split-infinitive prohibition is now null and void, we English teachers need to be informed so we will be free to pass the news on to our students and to boldly go into the uncertain future where no English teacher has gone before.

—*David R. Williams*

Letter to the *Washington Post*, published March 7, 1998.

that meant a state of perfect objectivity. Judges were supposed to be disinterested. Today it has come to mean "uninterested." But we already have a term for uninterested. We still need disinterested. But I cannot use it in its original meaning and expect to be understood. Most literate people fight stubbornly to retain the unique meaning of "unique." This word means one and only one. Therefore, you cannot have highly unique, very unique, more unique, or any of the other ways in which people use the word to mean "rare." We already have "rare"; let's keep "unique" unique.

"Hopefully," however, exists in that gray area between the snobs and the slobs. According to the grammar purists, "hopefully" is an adverb defining an action to be used only when an action is done with hope or in a hopeful manner, as in such sentences as "Hopefully, he took the exam" or "Hopefully, he bought a lottery ticket." But most slobs, and most of us are slobs, use it in place of "I hope." If I say, "Hopefully, I took the exam," wouldn't you answer, "Don't you know whether you did?" The sentence is ambiguous and can be read either way. William Safire, the author of the "On Language" column for the *New York Times* and one of the nation's leading experts on all things pertaining to the American use of words, is willing to let the original use of "hopefully" as an adverb be replaced by its use as a substitute for "I hope." In fact, he can do little to stop it. The change is here. But in English departments across the country, purists are fighting fiercely like King Canute to stem the oncoming tide. If you do not want to be a statistic in their struggle, be careful when you use "hopefully."

Adjective or Adverb?

Most students by the time they are in college know that an adjective describes a noun, a thing, and an adverb describes an action, how something is done, and that most adverbs end in "ly." The problem arises when the adverb does not end in "ly" and the writer is not sure which word is the adverb and whether in fact an adjective or an adverb is called for. One can only learn the exceptions that cause the most problems. Here are two of the worst.

To "do good" means to do good works. The noun defined by the adjective "good" is understood. To "do well" means to do in a good manner. In idiomatic American speech, it specifically means to be making money. If someone asks, "How are you?" and you answer, "I'm doing good," you are in fact saying you are involved in doing good works. If you want to say you are getting along okay, say, "I am doing well." My favorite phrase that helps to distinguish these is the statement often quoted about the Quakers: "They came to America to do good, and they did right well."

Even more troublesome is the "feeling bad" and "feeling badly" dilemma. This is a useful distinction to grab because it vividly illustrates the difference in meaning and hence the importance of knowing what you are saying. To "feel bad" is to feel sick; to "feel badly" is to have numb or clumsy hands and thus not do the act well. A difference exists between feeling clumsy and feeling clumsily. Simply remember the phrase "She felt bad because he felt badly." Or if you find that too sexist, substitute the gender pronouns of your choice.

The sign "Think Smart" is like the bumper sticker "Think Snow." Since "smart" is not an adverb, an implied "about" (as in "Think About Snow") is stuck in there. "Think Smartly" is what all of those stupid signs should say.

Prepositions and Their Pronouns

By now you are undoubtedly getting pretty irritated that I still haven't told you what those horrendous sinners did to bring down the wrath of Stanley Marcus, he of the "personal antipathy" to the misuse of the personal pronoun following a preposition. Well, here it is.

Prepositions always take the objective form of the pronoun. The objective form is the form when the pronoun is an object; the subjective is the way you would use it as a subject. Think of a simple sentence: "She shot him." "She" is the subject, the actor; "him" is the object, that to which the action was done. All prepositions take the objective form. For, with, between, to, by, into, out of, and so on, and so on, all take an objective pronoun. This is true even when there are two pronouns connected by a conjunction. Hence, Marcus's girlfriend should have said, "There is so much love between you and me," not "you and I." You wouldn't say "He shot I" would you? Of course not. The objective form is "me." There are still English teachers in fourth grades across the country who think it is always better to use "I" than to use "me." They are responsible for ruining that poor girl's life. Don't let them ruin yours.

Knowing whether a pronoun is the object or subject helps even in sentences without prepositions. Whether you should write "It is I" or "It is me" depends on who is kicking and whom is getting kicked. When the judge asks, "Who was smoking the joint?" you should answer, "It was I." When the judge asks, "Who got taken to jail after the cops broke down the door?" your girlfriend should respond, "It was me." Why? Because in the first example, "I" is the subject, the one doing the act. In the second example, the girlfriend was the object of police brutality, hence "me." This can be important. "My husband likes football better than me" suggests a divorce is imminent. "My husband likes football better than I" is merely a statement of preference for another sport.

An old, snob rule forbids the appearance of prepositions at the ends of sentences, and a few old profs may still abide by this antiquity. But decades ago, no less a master of the English language than Winston Churchill skewered this rule. A secretary going over the manuscript of his history of World War II changed a sentence that ended "put up with." In the margin, to emphasize the contortions that avoiding the construction would entail, Churchill wrote, "This is the sort of nonsense up with which I will not put!"

Fewer and Less

It may surprise you to learn that "fewer" and "less" aren't interchangeable, although they're so often used incorrectly that it seems as though they might be. If you become confused about which word to use, follow this simple rule: "Fewer" is for things you can count, and "less" is for things you can't, such as abstract ideas. Therefore, it would be "fewer elephants" but "less noise," "fewer dollars" but "less money," "fewer bigots" but "less hatred." All those illiterate signs in the supermarket should read,

"Express lane, ten items or fewer." Once you master the difference, the ability to make the correct distinction between "less" and "fewer" will immediately set you apart from the pack and help elevate you to the status of grammar guru.

Who and Whom

This is similar to the preposition problem. A sane, logical rule exists for when to use "who" and when to use "whom." "Who" is the subjective form; "whom" is the objective form. Thus, use "who" when the word is the subject; use "whom" when it is the object. "The girl whom he kissed" is good grammar, but so is "the boy who kissed her." The problem comes when the "who" phrase gets confused with its surrounding sentence. The rule is to take the "who" phrase out of context and examine it by itself to determine if the "who" is doing the acting or is being acted upon. "Good grades are possible for whoever deserves them." In this example, the preposition "for" immediately suggests to the ear that "whom" is needed. Didn't I just say in the section on prepositions that prepositions always take the objective form of the pronoun? Isn't "for" a preposition? And isn't "whom" the objective form? Yes to all three questions. *But* one must look at the "who" phrase and only the "who" phrase. "For whoever deserves them" is correct because in the phrase "whoever deserves them," "whoever" is the subject and "them" is the object. These can be tricky; watch out.

Even nastier is the "who" phrase that makes the "who" seem to be the object of the phrase when it isn't. If the sentence read "for whoever I think deserves them," doesn't "I" become the subject and "who" the object, making "whom" correct? No! Why not? Because "I think" is a parenthetical aside, an additional bit of information. "Deserves" is still the verb of the "who" phrase. Cute, eh?

And while we are "whoing," people, even cops, capitalists, and teachers are always "who," never "that" or "which."

Unclear Referents

These come in two flavors: pronouns that could refer to any one of a number of nouns, and pronouns that could refer to absolutely anything. "Whenever dogs bite people, they get put to death." To what does the "they" in this sentence refer? Is it the dogs or the people? The referent for "they" is unclear, and thus this dog of a sentence needs to be fixed. Either the dogs or the people should be put to death.

The pronoun "it" is too often used without any referent at all. This leaves to the imagination the job of figuring out what is being talked about. And since most people think about sex most of the time, the result is all those bumper stickers saying "Divers do it deeper," "Conservationists make it last longer," "Bakers make it rise," "Teachers do it in front of the class," or whatever your profession is. A furniture company in the Washington, D.C., area advertises "You'll love it at Levitz." Well, I love it, but I never considered doing it on one of the beds in the Levitz showroom. Nevertheless, in such advertising the use of the unclear referent "it" is a deliberate attempt to exploit the ambiguous potential of the word. When done deliberately like this, such use of "it" is clever; when done unintentionally, it is just stupid. Note the ambiguous "it" in the last line of the introduction to this book; am I referring to life or to grammar? Here, the ambiguity is intentional.

I, Me, Mine; I, Me, Mine; I, Me, Mine

Ms. Snigglebottom undoubtedly taught you never to use "I" but always to be objective. It is necessary at the high school level to pry students away from the endless contemplation of self and to get them to think about the world outside themselves. Adolescent writing can be painfully narcissistic. Hence, high school teachers forbid the use of "I" in order to control the excesses of adolescence. Once students have made it to college, however, things forbidden to them when they were children become real possibilities, even sometimes necessities. We teachers do want to know what you personally think. The purpose of your writing a paper on Jonathan Edwards is to show the world what Jonathan Edwards looks like from your unique perspective as a human being. Each one of us is different; some are white, some black, some male, some female, some Asian, some gay, most in fact a unique mixture of some of the above and more. Your paper is the expression of your unique viewpoint. What you then need is a balance of subjective opinion and objective fact. In high school, you were told to leave the "I" out and merely be objective. Now you need to bring the subjective "I" back into your analysis. You can do this without ever actually using the word "I" if that word becomes too bothersome. After writing "I believe that George Will is a pompous ass," edit out the "I believe that." We know the rest of the sentence is your opinion. Your subjective point of view is clearly present. Hence, you get the best of both worlds, subjective color and energy with objective language, logic, and fact. Even George Will would approve.

Subjunctive Dreams

The subjunctive is what grammarians call a "mood." It is an uncertain state of mind. Hence this form almost always follows a word like "if." If it were raining yesterday, would you have gotten wet? "Were" here is the subjunctive form. When my friend Meg proposed to her German boyfriend somewhat hesitantly, she asked him, "If I were to ask you to marry me, what would you say?" Her question was in the subjunctive; his answer was not. So she shifted from the subjunctive to future time and asked, "Okay, will you?" In the present tense, they are Herr and her.

The political extremist Lyndon LaRouche, who knows for certain that Henry Kissinger and the Queen of England are engaged in narcotics trafficking, insists on using the subjunctive even though he never had a doubt in his life. I once pointed out this peculiar inconsistency in a news column, and I was rewarded with a free copy of his writings from prison. The very first line says, "It were an ill wind which had not sent some Plato dialogues into my cell." It were too much for me.

Plurals

This problem should not even be listed here, except that I see it so often I must include it. The plural of words ending in "y" is "ies": my family but our families. The word most often so abused is "societies." If you want to make a possessive out of it, the singular is "society's" and the plural is "societies'." If a society has problems, then it is "society's problems." If many societies have problems, then write "societies' problems."

Speaking of plural societies, here is a good example of why words matter. Is the name of our country a singular or a plural noun? *Is* the United States a country, or *are* the United States separate parts of a country? Be careful how you answer this. The last time this issue was raised, half a million kids died horrible deaths.

A fellow teacher, James Stripes, begs me to include, if it is not already too late, the surprising news that when you use a plural noun, all of the referents to it must also be plural. Hence, "the children put their coats in the closet" and "the Pilgrim mothers cooked their turkeys in iron pots." Be sure you know what the subject of your sentence is. A colony of rats lives under the school, not "live." The colony is singular even if it has a million rats, except of course in England where a mob are plural.

Hyphens

These are probably underused. A hyphen in time can save you a great deal of embarrassment. Note that many of these technical problems are considered errors because they create confusion and ambiguity. They force the reader to stop and backtrack through the sentence to figure out what is being said. In a string of adjectives before a noun, each word is assumed to define the noun. Is a small dairy farmer a small person or a person who farms a small dairy? If you mean a farmer of small dairies, a hyphen between the two adjectives (small-dairy) makes your meaning clear. How about processed baby food? Yum!

English being at least part German allows the use of nouns as adjectives, but the abuse of this liberty, as any liberty, can become excessive. So too with the turning of nouns into verbs. Here, moderation is a virtue.

Note also at the end of the line that a hyphen can be used to separate a word too long to fit the space. Such a forced separation should occur only between syllables or if possible between a double consonant. Do this right. Show how intelligent you are.

Must of Alot of Attitude

I could of course go on forever, but let me leave this category with a lumpen collection of ugly errors. The verb form "must have" when contracted becomes "must've." To the ear, this sounds exactly like "must of." Writers who don't read don't know this and end up writing "must of" instead of "must've."

Though few have adopted the practice, I would like to leave as my legacy the introduction of the double contraction. We certainly say it, so we ought to be able to write it. It wouldn't've seemed so weird if we'd been doing it all along. I couldn't've made a better contribution if I'd solved the mind/body debate.

You lie down, but you lay an object down. Without an object of the verb, you lie alone. Although you lie down alone, you do lay your body down. The chicken lies down and then lays an egg. I have a magazine ad showing two bored guys and a girl watching TV. The caption underneath reads, "On January 1, you can lay around and watch football." Is that a stupid mistake? Or did the ad agency hope the readers would assume an unspoken object to lay?

A lot of students still think that "alot" is one word; it is not. And I despise the currently popular word "attitude" because it is so utterly meaningless. A student once wrote on a paper that in *Uncle Tom's Cabin*, Simon Legree "had an attitude problem." Surely, one can get more specific. A student complained once in class that my picking on her grammar showed that I had an attitude. I replied, "What kind of an attitude do you mean? Happy? Sad? Angry? Frustrated?" "Well," she said, putting her hand on her hip, "you certainly do have an attitude!"

14

"Punct'uation!?!"

Clueless High School Teachers

Punctuation does matter. Try adding the correct punctuation to the following string of words:

Woman without her man is useless.

If you didn't come up with "Woman! Without her, man is useless," a delegation from NOW is heading your way.

Most of you are not to blame for your pathetic punctuation skills. They are not your fault. You are all victims of society's neglect. The people I blame for most of the horrors I have to correct at the college level are not the few underpaid and overworked saints but the incompetent high school English teachers. Maybe they are not to blame either. Maybe they are the victims of some larger social trends that downplay the teaching of grammar in favor of empowerment and self-esteem. I treasure a memo passed around my department some years back in which we were encouraged to grade in blue or green instead of red because red was such an angry color. A friend of mine who has since left the profession was not allowed to teach grammar in his Fairfax, Virginia, high school English classes. Grammar, he was told, is organic; the students learn it by osmosis while reading great literature. When osmosis failed to take, he tried setting up an extracurricular grammar program outside of class for those who needed help. The superintendent of schools, no less, made him stop.

So when students tell me they had always been taught to use "who" when the subject is singular and "whom" when it is plural, I believe them. They are shocked, even angered, to be told that "alot" is not one word or that the use of "myself" when an objective "me" is perfectly okay makes them look like a complete fop. As one critic put it, "'Myself' is the refuge for idiots who were taught early that 'me' is a dirty word." The same idiots were taught by this same teacher that it is always more polite to say "I." It is not. Nor should a comma be placed every time you take a breath. I swear some of the students who hand in papers to me must be dying of asthma. But whether you are dying of asthma or the innocent victim of high school English teachers without a clue, someone must step into the chain of cause and effect at some point and fix the fault. Even if your crimes are not your "fault," they are your responsibility. Get it right.

Commas

The comma is a little cur that causes more problems than it should. Some basic rules help govern the use of the comma; once learned, these rules will work 90 percent of the time.

1. The most common comma error has to do with the use of the comma to separate two parts of a sentence. Recall the basics: A sentence must have both a subject and a verb; sometimes it has an object as well. If you have two such sentences connected by a conjunction like "and," then you must put in a comma before the connecting "and." Other such conjunctions include "but," "for," "yet," and "nor." If either of the sentences could not stand alone without the support of the other, then you do not put in the comma. For instance:

Mary kicked her boyfriend and then shot his dog.

In this sentence, "and then shot his dog" cannot stand alone as a sentence because it has no subject. The phrase depends upon the subject of the first sentence, Mary. Hence, no comma is put before "and."

Compare this example:

Mary kicked her boyfriend, and then she shot his dog.

The sentence "then she shot his dog" can stand alone. Hence, a comma is required before the "and."

In a more complicated sentence, you may have to stop and think to figure out if it has a subject. But that is the point: The writer must do that work so the reader will not have to. Anytime a reader is forced to reread a sentence to figure it out, the writer is doing a bad job. Consider this sentence:

Mary shot her boyfriend and his dog bit her.

If a comma isn't placed before "and," a reader would at first read the sentence to say that Mary shot her boyfriend and his dog. Then the reader would realize something was wrong and have to back up and read it again right. The writer has the responsibility to keep the reader informed by using correct punctuation as road signs to guide the reader.

2. The second most troublesome use of the comma comes when a phrase within a sentence has to be separated from the rest of the sentence. To many students, the distinction seems totally arbitrary. It is not. Consider this sentence:

My grandmother who smokes pot is eighty.

Would you or wouldn't you put commas around "who smokes pot"? The answer is that you can do either; it depends entirely on what you mean to say. That is the important reason for going to all this trouble. Including the commas changes the meaning. If you don't know that, it's as if you were writing in a foreign language you do not understand. Imagine the possibilities for disaster!

Without commas, this sentence says that of your two grandmothers it is the pot-smoking one who is eighty. (The bourbon-drinking one, presumably, is ninety-two.) Without commas, the phrase, as we say, is restrictive. It is there to indicate specifically which grandmother you are talking about.

With commas, "My grandmother, who smokes pot, is eighty" implies that you have only one grandmother, who is eighty and who (by the way) smokes pot. The commas separate out extra material that is added to the sentence but is not necessarily crucial to the main point, which is your grandmother's age. You could say "My grandmother is eighty," and the basics of the sentence would remain. You would, however, have just killed off your ninety-two-year-old bourbon-drinking grandmother. Way to go!

Another example of this same principle occurs when you are citing an author's books. Robert Frost's poem "Stopping by Woods on a Snowy Evening" is a well-loved poem. Writing it this way, without commas around the name of the poem, specifies which of Frost's many poems you are talking about. It is restrictive. If you put in commas and write "Robert Frost's poem, 'Stopping by Woods . . . ,'" you are saying that Robert Frost wrote only one poem, which (by the way) is called "Stopping by Woods . . . ." The difference between "Jane's husband Ted" and "Jill's husband, Fred," is that Jane is a bigamist. See?

The same principle applies elsewhere. "He stopped in Fairfax, Virginia, by mistake." Always put commas around the state or country so designated. This is because you are saying that Fairfax is (by the way) in Virginia. It is an extra bit of information like the year in the date July 4, 1776, when our country declared independence. I find that saying "(by the way)" to myself helps me to determine whether any particular phrase ought to or ought not to have commas around it.

For those who relish the finer distinctions, this is also the reason for sometimes using "that" and at other times using "which." You use "which" when the information in the phrase is incidental to the main idea, and you put a comma before the "which." You use "that" when the information is important and restricts the meaning of the main thought; in this case no comma is used. When you use "which," you should be able to think "(by the way)."

3. Things in a series require commas: "he, she, and I." Some teachers allow the second comma to be omitted; not I. It is

there to avoid confusion. Use it. (Regrettably, most journalists don't.) Also, in a list of adjectives before a noun, if the word "and" can be inserted but is not, substitute a comma: "the green, ugly, scum-covered lake." Such rules are not as arbitrary and pointless as they seem. Not too long ago, a millionaire left his fortune to his children, "Brad, Joe and Suzie." The lawyer administering the estate gave half the money to Brad, the other half to Joe and Suzie. Joe and Suzie sued claiming that daddy meant to leave an equal third to each. The judge looked at the punctuation and ruled otherwise. We cannot know the intention of the author, especially when he is dead; we only know what the author wrote.

This rule applies just as well in other cases. When Vachel Lindsay chanted

> Death is an Elephant,
> Torch-eyed and horrible,

the emphasis is on the image of the elephant being torch-eyed and horrible, not death. Frost's famous line "The woods are lovely, dark and deep" is much better without the comma before the "and." With the comma, as some versions have it, "lovely," "dark," and "deep," all define the woods equally. Without the comma, "dark and deep" become a quality of loveliness. Police in Baltimore recently killed a murderer who had taken a boy hostage. As the *Post*'s article put it, "The SWAT team burst into the tiny row house, killed Palczynski as he allegedly stirred and saved the boy." Who saved the boy? According to the *Post*, without a second comma before the "and," credit has to go to Palczynski and not to the police. So be careful out there.

4. Introductory and final phrases which (whoops! should be "that") might cause confusion or create ambiguity should have commas: "Heading for the green, Dad forgot his golf clubs." Note that without the comma the reader would automatically read "Heading for the green Dad . . ." In the same category, note the difference between a "new hip joint" and a "new, hip joint." Which one would you get from your doctor?

5. Other uses of the comma include

- a direct address when the person's name or title is included: "Love me, daddy, all night long."
- before a quotation: He said, "My heart is aflame or maybe it's gas."
- contrasted elements set aside: "I asked for a piece of pie, not pizza pie, when I called."

Note that in all of these, the underlying rule is to avoid ambiguity and confusion. Use the least amount of punctuation needed to keep your meaning clear. If you are not sure if you need a comma, try to imagine how another reader might misunderstand your intent if the commas were left out.

Semicolons

My best advice on semicolons is not to use them or use them with great care. I rarely see them used correctly on college papers. Faulkner could not have written without them. But you are not Faulkner, and Faulkner was not writing for a college class.

If you must know, used correctly the semicolon substitutes for a period to join two closely related ideas. In other words, it should not be used to set off phrases at either end of a sentence that could not otherwise stand alone as independent sentences. So why not use a period? "I am going to the library; Jill is going to the market" is an example of the proper use of a semicolon. "Jill is going to the market; the one near the end of town" is an example of the incorrect use of a semicolon. I most often see semicolons connecting two phrases that are joined in contrast to each other; however, this convention is overused.

Phrases in a series also take semicolons instead of commas if there are commas within the phrases. This helps to separate the things that are being serialized from the extraneous information. For instance, when I am grading papers, I like to sit in a chair, a green one; to use a red pen, preferably a felt-tip; and to torture small animals, either hamsters or mice.

Colons

I always think of these two dots as two hands outstretched, palms up, saying "and here they are." Colons are thus used to introduce an itemized list or a quotation that is not otherwise introduced. "Many things are found in the sea: clams, mermaids, and hospital syringes." But if you have a phrase like "such as" introducing the list, you do not use the colon. The colon takes the place of the introductory phrase. In a quotation, the same distinction applies. "Emerson said, 'A foolish consistency is the hobgoblin of little minds.'" But "There is an Emersonian phrase that is much quoted: 'A foolish consistency is the hobgoblin of little minds.'" In the second example, the colon can be thought of as saying "and here it is."

Quotation Marks

The rule regulating the use of quotation marks is fairly straightforward: Put quotation marks around only actual, literal quotations. Some students have begun to use quotation marks for emphasis; off with their heads! Use the double quotation marks only on either side of a statement that you can prove is a quotation, word for word. If the original is ungrammatical or misspelled, quote it exactly. If you want to protect yourself from the charge that you left in a typo that in fact is not yours, put [*sic*] in brackets after the quoted word. This is Latin for "so." It means, "Hey, prof, this author actually said it this way. It's not my fault. And I've got the proof if you need it." Note that parentheses within a quote are considered part of the quote. Only brackets indicate an intrusion into the quotation.

A case was argued in the courts recently in which a writer had enclosed in quotation marks words not actually said in an unflattering book about a man who subsequently sued the author. A lot of writers who should know better defended the practice on the grounds that the distinction between fact and fiction is so subjective that it does not matter. This is an example of the literary world's desire to believe that language, its language, constitutes reality, that there is no truth outside of language, and since all such "truth" is really a language construction, then any language construction is as good as any other. The courts decided otherwise, bless them.

The biggest problem I've run into with quotation marks on student papers is placement of any punctuation not part of the quote. Once upon a time, the rule regulating this was easy to follow. All punctuation went within the quotation marks whether it was part of the quotation or not. Did Nixon really say, "I am not a crook?" Note that the question mark was not part of the quote, but still it was placed inside the quotation marks. The only exceptions to this rule were the colon and the semicolon. Absolutely everything else went inside the quotation marks no matter what the circumstances.

You undoubtedly have noticed the nervous use of the past tense in this explanation. During the year I was in Slovakia imparting the glories of American culture to the victims of Marxism, someone changed the rules on me. I still have not figured out who or why.

But the latest editions of the college handbooks have allowed question marks not part of the quotation to go outside of the quotation marks. Hence, my example above now should be written, Did Nixon really say, "I am not a crook"? I have been told that this change follows the change in printing technology from mechanical presses to computerized printing. When hot type was used, little letters made of lead were covered with ink to imprint the letters on paper, but the ink often would not cover the lonely little punctuation marks outside of the quotations. So the word went forth that henceforth all punctuation must go inside the quotation marks to satisfy the needs of the machines of production. Marx would've loved it. But what once was required in printing can now be changed. Printers no longer use hot type but instead use computers, and computers can do anything. Hence, the old rule may be changed in favor of more rational considerations. The Brits, I am told, have made punctuation follow rational meaning. We Americans have compromised. Periods and commas still stay within the quotation marks even if not part of the quotation, but exclamation points, question marks, and other assorted marks not part of the quotation do their business outside. This is another example of how our language is constantly changing. In American culture, nothing ever remains the same. Prepare to be flexible and stay tuned.

Note also that a quote within a quote gets single quote marks to distinguish it from the surrounding quotation. This is the only instance in which single quote marks are to be used. For some reason, more and more students are using single quote marks by themselves within their papers, perhaps because newspaper headline writers do. I don't know why. But it's wrong.

Finally, words when referred to as words, like the word "word," get put in quotation marks.

Parentheses (), Brackets [], and Dashes —

All of these are overused.

Parentheses are used to insert material into the text that is out of context. Most of the time, such material should either be omitted entirely or brought into the text in its own sentence or paragraph if it is important enough. Students too often use this device to jam extra information into the text in the hope that quantity will outweigh quality in the grade book. It won't.

Brackets are used primarily to insert material into the middle of a quote that is not part of the quote. If Cotton Mather has some brief line of Greek and you want to include your translation within the quote, then put your translation directly after the Greek in brackets. Otherwise, don't use brackets.

Emily Dickinson used dashes instead of punctuation. But she was not writing either for publication or for a college assignment. Besides, she was crazy. Students who use dashes are either indulging in a lazy habit or trying to show off. Often, I cannot tell if the mark is a dash or a hyphen. Rather than separating words, these actually connect them. The point of a college paper is to prove that you know how to do it right. Strictly speaking, dashes perform the same function as parentheses, so play it straight and use regular punctuation. Plenty of opportunities to be creative will occur if you graduate.

If you must insert parenthetical information in dashes, do so sparingly, and if your word-processing program won't create the long dash (—), use double hyphens--like this--so that someone won't read the words as "use double hyphens-like."

15

Citing Sources Successfully

MLA Style

Here we get into the tedious and technical yet necessary business of citing your facts and quotations. The rules have changed since I was in college, and some of my colleagues have not kept up. Therefore, not all of your professors in the humanities will expect the same system. Be sure to inquire before handing in your term research paper. The newer system is known as the MLA (Modern Language Association) system, and it is the one I recommend here. History departments seem to be the last place using the old superscript system, which involves putting a little raised number[1] that refers either to a footnote at the foot of the page, as here, or to an endnote at the end of the paper. All other humanities departments use the MLA style. The sciences use the APA style described in the next section. The differences are only in the method of citing a text, not in quoting it.

When quoting an author, put exact quotes in quotation marks. Nixon did not say "that he was not a crook." He said, "I am not a crook." If the original has a misspelled word or other mistake, quote it exactly as it appears anyhow, but put [*sic*] in brackets right after the mistake. Titles of published books, newspapers, magazines, and movies all get italicized. So do foreign words (like the *sic* here), musical compositions, plays, paintings, sculp-

---

[1] David R. Williams, *Sin Boldly! Dr Dave's Guide to Writing the College Paper*, (Perseus Publishing 2000), 187.

tures, ships, and trains. The common thread is that all these works can stand alone. Parts of larger works, such as titles of chapters or poems in a collection, get put in quotation marks.

Stick to the source you are using. If you are quoting from a separately published edition of Emerson's *Nature*, italicize it. If you are quoting from the reprint of "Nature" in an anthology, put it in quotation marks but italicize the name of the anthology. In the bad old days before computers, typewriters were unable to italicize, at least until the IBM Selectrics came along, and even then you had to change typing balls. So underlining, which had always been the proofreader's mark to the printer indicating the need to italicize, became a common substitute. Today, having reached the apex of perfection, we no longer need substitutes, so unless you are typing on a Smith-Corona, italicize.

First, all direct quotations must be cited. Anytime you use another person's exact words, you must acknowledge the citation. Block quotes are the most common example. Anytime you quote more than four typed lines of prose, you must separate the quotation from the rest of your text. Such block quotes are not surrounded with quotation marks. You must also be judicious. Don't pad your paper with lengthy block quotes that fill up half the page. Leave a blank line before and after the block. Leave ten spaces on the left but no extra spaces on the right. The citation goes at the end of the block outside of the period. Better than the padding of a series of block quotes is the excision of pithy phrases from within that quote that are then included within your text and not blocked. When possible, the citation to a quote within the text goes at the end of the sentence, but if there is any possibility of confusion, put the citation right after the quote, within the sentence rather than at its end.

Quotations, of course, are not the only things that need to be cited, but they are the most frequent. If you use an idea that someone else is responsible for, you must cite it. If you use a fact that might be questioned, even if you do not put anything in quotes, you should cite it. On the other hand, if you use facts or ideas that no one will question, don't bother citing them. This is a subjective decision that you must make. But if you say in your text that Dan Quayle was a member of the Communist Party in his youth, you had better provide a citation so we can check your sources.

Be sure to use credible sources relevant to your subject, and do not depend on one book or one particular point of view. You may have picked up a book by some paranoid LaRouchie or worse. Know your sources and what their biases are. I once had a student turn in a paper on arms control in which every footnote was a reference to some speech by Phyllis Schlafly, the right-wing harpy who helped to defeat the Equal Rights Amendment by traveling around the country giving speeches saying women belong in the home. I flunked him. If writing about the Arab-Israeli struggle, do not use books by Arabs or Israelis exclusively. Do not write about South Africa without taking into account books by Afrikaaners. Include several views. Do not depend upon any one source to provide unbiased accounts of its opponents.

Be sure to have in your variety of sources both primary and secondary materials. Primary materials are firsthand accounts, actual letters or documents. Secondary sources are books or articles that discuss and present the primary documents. Most of the texts college students have access to are secondary, but the Internet has made primary material more readily accessible. Do not simply quote books about Malcolm X. Find some published copies of his speeches or letters and read them yourself. Be sure also to have a mix of categories, not all books, all journal articles, all letters, or all WWW sources but some of each.

The citation itself requires the name of the author and the number of the page on which the quotation can be found. This information appears within parentheses and without punctuation. A line from Smith's *History of Virginia* might be followed by (Smith 13), with the quotation mark at the end of the quote before the first parenthesis. Leave out commas, p.'s, or any other unnecessary trivia. The idea is to provide the least amount of information in the text that will allow the reader to find the citation in the back of your paper on the "Works Cited" page.

The "Works Cited" page is basically a bibliography. There, all of the works you used or cited or both are listed alphabetically by the authors' last names. Hence, the reader ought to be able to skim down the first column on the page through the last names until the name "Smith" appears. If there is only one Smith, then the entire citation for that book should be there. The reader already knows that the quote is from page 13. If there are two books by the same Smith, then the writer needs to add information in the parentheses that will most quickly make the distinction clear. The first word of the two titles if different should do it. Hence, the citation might have to read (Smith *History* 13) as opposed to (Smith *Cooking* 33). If there are two different books by two different Smiths, the citation will have to include the first name as well as the last to make the distinction. The citation then might read (Smith, John 13) as opposed to (Smith, Tim 22). Whatever gets the reader to the right citation the fastest is correct.

Note that the punctuation falls outside the parentheses. The point of the parentheses is to separate the information from the surrounding sentence; it is thus within that sentence. A citation at the end of a sentence has a period to the right (Williams 190). Question marks also should go to the right. I have, however, seen cases even in the handbooks where a question mark came before the parentheses, but even these were followed by a period after the parentheses to make it clear which sentence the parentheses were within.

On the "Works Cited" page, simply list the works in alphabetical order by the last name of the author. Give the full title (italics for books, quotation marks for articles, and so on), the publisher, the publication date of the exact copy of the text you cited from, and the city of publication. Here are two examples of entries for the "Works Cited" page; the first is an article, the second a book:

Smith, Paul, and Janet Davis. "The Psychedelic Properties of Fermented Bat Guano." *Altered States Review* 10:4–40.
Williams, David R. *Sin Boldly! Dr. Dave's Guide to Writing the College Paper.* Cambridge: Perseus, 2000.

The reason for the citation is to allow a suspicious professor to check on your citation. You must therefore refer to the exact edition. The wording sometimes changes. Scholars are always finding new evidence of authorial intent that was mangled by some ham-handed or prudish printer. Even such classics as Emerson's *Nature* and Twain's *Huckleberry Finn* have recently undergone change.

There are too many variables in this format to list here. For all of the many possibilities, refer to a standard handbook, preferably *The MLA Style Manual.* Newspaper articles, encyclopedias, film and videotape, and other miscellaneous sources all have different rules for citation. If you remember the reason for the citation, you will probably not get in trouble. Provide the reader with a way to get from the quotation in the text to the actual source as quickly and easily as possible. That is all.

One problem I have with the MLA system is that it does not allow for an easy and consistent use of what I call "chatty endnotes." Sometimes we writers want to put extraneous information in a note and not in the text. For instance, we may want to thank our spouses and children for not interrupting us so that we could write our precious monographs. Or we might want to cite thirteen other books on the topic that failed to get the point. Or we might want to include some special pleading. All of these are legitimate and fun. I have read several academic books in which such footnotes were the only good parts. In this case, you need to create a second page titled "Notes." In your text, when you want to refer to one of these asides, you must use the old superscript 1, 2, 3, and so on. This is clumsy and makes the MLA system more complex rather than simpler. It imposes a second overlay of notation upon your text. Perhaps you should simply leave chatty footnotes to chatty professors, and either leave out the information if it is unimportant or include it in your text.

The MLA system is relatively new and still under development. In American English, nothing is ever written in stone. Be sure to ask your professor what he or she prefers. For instance, unlike the MLA, I see no reason to include a lengthy bibliography that basically duplicates the "Works Cited" page. I tell students to include each of their reference works on the "Works Cited" page even if they do not have a citation to it. But I also tell them to change its name to a "Works Consulted" page. That way, this page can serve as a bibliography too without having to lie about it. Why waste paper?

APA Style

The sciences tend to refer primarily to published papers, and these are indicated by the last name of the author and the date of the publication. Thus, for the APA style, created by the American Psychological Association, the citation in the text in parentheses will have the author's name, paper date, and page numbers with the p.'s; an example is (Smith, 1998, pp. 3–7). The citation will vary depending on the source(s): two authors (Smith and Jones, 1998, p. 2); three or more authors (Smith et al., 1998, p. 3); more than one reference (Smith, 1998; Jones, 1998; Magillicutty, 1923). If the author has already been named in the text, then the date alone is needed. Page numbers are needed only for direct quotations or specific facts. General references to a study need only the name and year. If a writer has more than one article in a given year, then each gets a different subset letter (Smith, 1998a) as opposed to (Smith, 1998b). As with the MLA style, if there are more than two Smiths who have published articles that you are referring to, use (Smith, P., 1998) to distinguish the citation from (Smith, Q., 1998). In case of a reference within a reference, both go in the parentheses (Smith, 1998, cited by Jones, 1999).

On the "Works Cited" page, the information is the same as with the MLA system, but it is presented differently. The authors are listed in alphabetical order by last name, but the first names are indicated only by initials, followed by the publication date, which is followed by the title. Nor are there underlinings, italics, or quotations marks to distinguish the titles of articles or books. Books get only publication places and publishers. Articles get simply the title of the article followed by the name of the magazine or journal, followed by the volume and number of the journal and ending with the page numbers. Hence, a journal citation might appear like this:

Smith, P., and J. Davis. 1998. The Psychedelic Properties of Fermented Bat Guano. Altered States Review. 10:4–40.

Millions of variants exist, of course. And to list them all would be impossible if not maddening. For your specific problem, check out one of the tedious writing handbooks hyped in every college bookstore. You can make notes on a piece of paper and return the book to the shelf without paying a cent. Other than that, remember to include the information needed to guide the reader to the specific text or article you got your information from. If an additional bit of data seems helpful, do not be afraid to add it. Not even scientists are so anal that they will mark you down for a misplaced comma in a citation.

Citing Cyberspace

No generally accepted style yet exists for how to write citations for the World Wide Web, e-mail, or any of the other aspects of the Internet. One of the first problems is that the purpose of your citation is to let the reader find your source. Books in the library are assumed to stay there, even to be found in more than one library. But websites come and websites go. No one can guarantee that the website will still exist, or exist at the address at which you found it. I recommend to my students that in addition to putting in the citation the date they found the website information, they should make a hard copy of any really controversial part in case I challenge it and the website they cited has disappeared.

The approach to citing cyberspace ought to follow the same principles of all other citations. Get the reader to the site with the necessary information as quickly as possible.

Most websites have titles if not authors. These can often be found at the top of the page. If an author's name exists, by all means put it first. If not, put the title of the article or page first. Then cite any information about the source of the site, what organization is behind it, or what person. Finally, give the entire URL, the lengthy Web address beginning with http://. If a book or magazine article is being cited from the Web, cite it just as you would a book or magazine article in hard copy, but add the URL at the end of the citation with the date on which it was read immediately before the URL.

For instance, I have on my website an unpublished paper I read at a pop-culture conference on Thelma, Louise, and

Jonathan Edwards. The citation to it in the "Works Consulted" would appear so:

Williams, David R. "Thelma and Louise in the Wilderness or Butch Cassidy and Jonathan Edwards in Drag." 2/10/00. http://mason.gmu.edu/~drwillia/thelma.html.

A million variations exist here too, and for most of them, you are on your own. Numerous books exist, but if you are consistent and use common sense, you ought to be able to figure out what is the minimum you can get away with. If not, check out these websites: for MLA style, http://www.mla.org/set_stl.htm, and for the APA, http://www.apa.org/journals/webref.html.

16

A Sample Quiz— Just for Fun!

Each of the following sentences, most of which came from papers I have graded, has some problem or problems. Locate the error and correct the sentence. Then, and only then, look at the next page for the real poop.

1. Southpaws, who are superstitious, will not pitch on Fridays.
2. College students who do not write well flunk English.
3. As a student, Aunt Normies' dinners are to be avoided.
4. What we need are some engineers broken down by their specialties.
5. As a boy games of war are fun.
6. We drove to Reno Nevada to gambol.
7. Doug is the only one of the boys who always stand straight.
8. She wasn't aloud to have friends over their house.
9. Emersons poem Brahma can be found in his book Selected Poems.
10. Hopefully, you will pass the test, otherwise I will feel badly.
11. Whom should I say is calling?
12. If their taking there car their, they'd better have a credit card handy.
13. By engine tune-ups, by keeping his tires filled, and by driving carefully, his mileage was increased.

14. A clever dog knows it's master.
15. Literally climbing the walls, I scream as another misplaced modifier appeared on the term paper and I decided to immediately give up teaching, and became a sadistic killer.

1. This sentence says that all southpaws are superstitious. Unless this is what the author intended, the "who" clause should not be set off by commas but should be restrictive.
2. This sentence is probably correct. To surround the "who" phrase with commas would be to say "College students, who (by the way) do not write well, . . ." But a few college students do write well, even today, so the sentence is better as it stands.
3. This is a classic MM. Aunt Normie's dinners are not "a student." Nor should there be an apostrophe after the s unless her name is Normies, which I doubt.
4. Are the engineers being broken down? That is what the sentence says. What we need is a list of engineers, and the list needs to be broken down by the engineers' specialties. Use idioms correctly.
5. This is another MM. The games are not "a boy."
6. "Nevada" needs to be separated out by commas, and "gambol" should probably be "gamble." But who knows? What you mean is up to you.
7. The word "stand" should be "stands." Common sense says that Doug is the one who stands straight, not that he is the only one (what?) of a group of boys all of whom stand straight.
8. "Aloud" is misspelled; the word is "allowed." The phrase "over their house" suggests that her friends are birds. This is a colloquialism the language could do without.
9. "Emersons" should be "Emerson's." "Brahma" should be in quotation marks but should not be surrounded with commas. The title of the book tells you Emerson had more than one poem, so leaving "Brahma" free of commas discriminates which poem. The title of the book should be in italics. Put a comma in front of the title only if it is the only book he wrote. It's not.

10. "Hopefully" is always a problem; use it at your risk. The second comma is a classic comma splice holding two separate sentences together. Use a semicolon or a period. And to "feel badly" means to be clumsy with your hands. It should say "feel bad."

11. Gotcha! The "should I say" is a secondary clause. The "who" phrase is "Who is calling?" Hence, "Who should I say is calling?" is correct. It isn't "whom should I say?" as if "whom" were the object of "say."

12. "If their" becomes "If they are." "Their" is the possessive, so "there car" should be "their car." And "there" is the place.

13. Parallelism is the problem here. The first of the three phrases should agree with the other two: "By keeping his engine tuned." Nor did "his mileage" do all these things. He did. So use the active, not the passive, voice and eliminate the misplaced modifier.

14. If you take your dog for a walk every time it goes to the door and whimpers, then "it's" is correct for it is the master. Otherwise if you are its master, then it's "its."

15. Do not say "literally" unless you are a fly; in fact, don't say it even if you are. The tenses here need to be made consistent. If "scream" is left in, then "appeared" must be put in the present tense also, as must "decided" and "became." Thus, "scream . . . decide . . . become . . . ." Since these are two complete sentences joined by a conjunction, "and," there should be a comma after "paper." If you want to leave the comma out, eliminate the "I" also. "To immediately give up" is a split infinitive. The comma after "teaching" is inappropriate since the final phrase cannot stand alone as an independent clause.

17

Concluding Sermon

Try to remember and believe that the purpose of writing is to communicate ideas as clearly and as quickly as possible. Do not try to show off or confuse or pontificate. Do not be afraid to let your ideas stand boldly and clearly on the page. Writers who clothe their ideas in layers of elaborate silk and satin are hiding the reality underneath, not beautifying it. Away with their verbal fig leaves!

All of those postmodern theorists who try to confuse you with their denial of any known truth (except theirs) are playing games with their minds. Don't let them play games with yours. You may think yourself incapable of thinking and writing at the sophisticated level of these clever pedants. But even if you are crazy, you are no crazier than the average asshole sitting on a tenured throne. Nor should you be ashamed of your beliefs however much the theorists try to persuade you to believe that there is nothing to believe but their belief in nonbelief.

Being something of an old-fashioned essentialist myself, I am naive enough to believe that outside of the virtual-reality language helmets we all wear, something exists. That something, whatever it is, call it reality or truth or the force, Allah or God, may not be anything like our artificial socially constructed selves imagine. But it is the context out of which we arose and within which we live and move and have our being. Our perceptions of that reality may be distorted and blocked by our virtual-reality language helmets. We may all be trapped within the matrix. Deus may be absconditus. But S/He/It is still out there somewhere, still handsomer than the affectation of love. The goal is not just to make our virtual-reality cages more comfortable or equitable but to break out somehow, someday, and be free in Zion.

Remember that we are all sinners, naked before God; none of us really knows the answers. We are all groping in the dark. Academic tyrants and bullies will try to pretend that they know, that they are superior beings entrusted with some secret Truth. They will try to terrorize you into lies and confusion. Don't let them. Of course you might be and probably are wrong, but so are they. So speak your own ideas with clarity. Emerson at least had the right approach: "To believe that what is true for you in your private heart is true for all men; that is genius. Speak your latent conviction and it shall be the universal sense." Therefore, Sin Boldly! Stand fast in the liberty of the spirit and be not entangled again in the yoke of bondage.

THE AUTHOR'S RAP SHEET

After almost getting expelled for exposing his prep school's outrages in the Boston press, **David Williams** spent 1968 crossing the Pacific in the merchant marine and fighting the Vietnam War in the peace movement. Wanted in Oregon for jaywalking, he hitchhiked home to enjoy the mayhem of the Sixties at Harvard where he occasionally attended classes. After a lost postgraduate year, still unexplained, he entered Harvard Divinity School to determine the meaning of the word "God." Chosen Baccalaureate speaker, he preached a jeremiad that caused one professor to goose-step off the stage in protest. He later got married, fathered two sons, Nathan and Sam, and entered the American Civ Program at Brown where his weekly column offended every faction on campus. He ended up in Virginia working in a vineyard and teaching full time as a "part-time" college professor at George Mason University where he was honored with the year 2000 "Teaching Excellence Award." Escaping from the Marxists in the English Department, he spent a Fulbright year in Slovakia confirming his hosts' suspicions about Americans. Back home, his wife replaced him with an unemployed redneck and his university passed him over for more politically-correct hirelings. He now lives in Swampoodle, an abandoned black community in a Virginia swamp, writing, grading sophomore papers, and brewing his own bitter beer.